GRACED
BEYOND TELLING

While our contemporary society is increasingly secular, there is growing interest in exploring and deepening personal spirituality – this is a book for our times. *Graced Beyond Telling*, Corrie's account of her life-long spiritual journey, offers a 'lighthouse' for those on this voyage of discovery. I highly recommend her engaging account of God working in her life.

Gabrielle McMullen AM

Graced Beyond Telling is a love story of great depth, beauty and honesty as Corrie shares both the outer and inner journey of her life and call. Based on her personal journal writings of forty years, it holds together light and darkness, dislocation and connection, adventure and ordinariness, pain and delight, wonder and struggle. Laced through these paradoxes is a resilience of spirit and a profound openness of heart to a God who is always present – even in seeming absence. Corrie's story is a story of responding again and again to the ever-deepening call to be all that she can be as she grows deeply into her very essence ... in God. From this place of essence, she is able to respond to all the outer needs that her unique set of gifts enables her to serve. Her story speaks to our own stories, 'massaging' them into life again and again. It did for me! Thank you for sharing this very intimate story with us all.

Madeline Duckett rsm
Spiritual director, retreat facilitator
author of three books
foundress of the Contemplative Evolution Network.

Sister Corrie's extensive experience in a variety of ministries in her religious congregation and her wide reading and study are rich resources for her writing. Moreover, Corrie reflects on her experience with an acute sensitivity to God's presence and invitation in her life.

The 'dark journey' of her subtitle is no sinister darkness. I hear it, rather, as a reference to our inability to see the way ahead when we are in the dark. In one of many self-revealing chapters, Corrie says: 'I feel lost, without any sense of direction' (p 42), a statement that permeates subsequent chapters. These are the times when we are called to trust and wait on God, 'to rest in the Silence' (p 177). Doing that, Corrie discovers grace – grace 'beyond telling' – even in the painful times and the apparent darkness:

> Emptiness is the womb of fullness, darkness is the womb of light, silence is the womb of sound. (p 177)

Brian Gallagher msc
Author, *The Joy of Ageing*

Graced Beyond Telling is a beautiful exploration and sharing of Corrie van den Bosch MSS's inner spiritual life and the interplay between this and her life's journey as a Missionary Sister of Service. It is raw, honest and heartwarming as she shares many of her intimate journal entries. I was inspired to reflect upon my own memories and spiritual journal. From the beginning, I was captivated and moved; and found myself unable to put the book down. In fact, as soon as I'd finished, I wanted to re-read the book. This is a book with heart and soul; and offers an invitation to delve more deeply into the hope and grace that is offered to all.

Fiona Basile, journalist
Author, *Shhh ... God is in the Silence*
and *Immense*

A Soul's Dark Journey

GRACED
BEYOND TELLING

Corrie van den Bosch

COVENTRY
PRESS

Published in Australia by
Coventry Press
33 Scoresby Road
Bayswater VIC 3153

ISBN 9781922589415

Copyright © (2023) Missionary Sisters of Service

All rights reserved. Other than for the purposes and subject to the conditions prescribed under the *Copyright Act*, no part of this publication may be reproduced, stored in a retrieval system, or transmitted in any form or by any means, electronic, mechanical, photocopying, recording or otherwise, without the prior permission of the publisher.

Most Scripture quotations are from *The Jerusalem Bible* © 1966 by Darton Longman & Todd Ltd and Doubleday and Company Ltd; and from *The Revised New Jerusalem Bible*, copyright © 2018, 2019 by Darton, Longman & Todd, Ltd. Reprinted by Permission.

Catalogue-in-Publication entry is available from the National Library of Australia
http://catalogue.nla.gov.au

Cover design by Ian James – www.jgd.com.au
Cover photograph by Corrie van den Bosch
Text design by Coventry Press
Set in EB Garamond

Printed in Australia

Contents

Prelude: Graced beyond telling — 7

Part I   Beginnings — 9

Part II   Blossoming into a wider world — 13

1   Beyond the garden gate — 14
2   A life-changing experience — 18
3   The revealing power of words — 20
4   . . . And her name is Corrie — 23
5   The extraordinary ordinary — 27

Part III   Journey through chaos — 31

1   Disintegration — 32
2   Journey through chaos — 36
3   With no other light — 42
4   This is my body — 45
5   Drawn into crucified love — 48

Part IV   The Red Centre — 55

1   Transitions — 56
2   Becoming embedded in country — 58
3   Back to my roots — 61
4   Women's business — 67

5	The bread of wisdom	75
Part V	**To know and be known**	**79**
1	The world of dreams	80
2	Opening a box of worms	88
3	Until I see: awakening to the cosmos	92
4	Expanding consciousness	97
5	A spark of the Divine	100
6	Feed them with your flesh	104
Part VI	**A new millennium**	**109**
1	Dispossession	110
2	The healing power of forgiveness	115
3	The priceless pearl	122
4	The God who disappears	125
5	The awesome mission of being human	131
6	The BEholder	138
7	Lay your eggs and move on	145
Part VII	**Dying to Live**	**151**
1	Living in an evolving universe	152
2	Drawn toward the future	163
3	Love does such things	170
4	Unfinished symphony	179
Postscript: Gratitude		182
Appendix: The Missionary Sisters of Service story		185

Prelude
Graced beyond telling

Somewhere on the Hay Plains, a young woman stands alone on a claypan. She takes in her surroundings: nothing breaks the even line where land meets the vast dome of sky. She listens. No sound disturbs the profound silence pervading the landscape. She feels naked, infinitesimally small, in the vastness of space. And yet... She senses a subtle radiance: a *Presence* who knows her, enfolds her, penetrates her and permeates all that surrounds her. She is safe. She belongs. She is home. A sense of wonder fills her.

A few years later, the young woman is in the Philippines. She is travelling on a bus in Manila. As it inches its way across a congested intersection, she looks up the side street: a mass of people crowds it, all going about their business. Suddenly, her eyes are opened: each person in that seething mass of humanity is enfolded in that *Presence*, is known and embraced personally, whether or not he or she is aware of it, just as it embraced her on the Hay Plain: one embrace holding all. A sense of wonder fills her.

Years pass. It is Easter Sunday morning. The young woman is walking home from Mass along a suburban street. She is weeping, broken, lost in deep darkness, desolate, bereft. Nothing within her makes sense. Where is that *Presence* now? As she walks and weeps, Something draws her attention. What is it? She feels her way through her tears, through the desolate darkness. She becomes aware of a tenderness in her heart; *Something/Someone* is holding her heart. The sense is so subtle, she almost misses it. It is holding her with infinite tenderness. A profound peace radiates from that holding. It seeps into every part of her. The *Presence* knows her, knows her as she is, in her brokenness, in her lostness. She is safe. She belongs. She is home. Easter dawns. A sense of wonder fills her.

This woman took up journal writing in her later thirties. Her journal helped her explore and articulate what was going on within her – movements she could access only as she listened deeply for the words that could express her inner experience. In her journals, she frequently addressed God, pouring out her confusion, pain, anger, lostness, abandonment, or whatever she was feeling at the time. Writing gave her insight into herself, her reactions, her projections, her hopes and aspirations. She began to recognise recurring patterns and what evoked those patterns. She began to identify her vulnerabilities and her need for conversion and healing. Through her writing, she also began to recognise the leadings of the Spirit in her life.

The young woman, now no longer young, has pondered long and deep on the Mystery she encountered in her 80-plus years. Frequently, her journey took her into long stretches of desolate darkness, sometimes – just sometimes – momentarily lightened by experiences such as those described above. Yet even in times of darkness, full of fears and anxieties, she dimly knew there was an inner compass, a *Yes*, that kept her on her pathless path.

This book is the story of that *Yes*. It is more than her story. It is a story of God's grace, of the joys and griefs, the living and dying of daily experience, and of discovering herself part of a world infinitely larger than herself. Hers is just one precious moment in the life of a Universe that counts its years in billions. It is the story of the Spirit of Jesus the Christ, leading her inexorably to that final destination, the heart of our Triune God.

Part I

Beginnings

On an autumn morning in 1939, in a village in the Netherlands, a child was born, the second in what would become a family of ten. That afternoon, she was baptised in the village church and inscribed in the parish register. It was a quiet ritual as was the custom in that place and time. Only the father and godparents were present.

In contrast to that almost hidden event, the Second World War had begun to unleash its terror on Europe. Very soon, its destructive arms would reach every continent of the world. Five years later, its fury abated, leaving some seventy-five million people dead and countless grieving and uprooted families. Our family and home survived; but my earliest memories are of those dark times.

We grew up in a faith-centred environment: morning and night prayer, grace before and after meals, pictures and statues of Jesus and Mary decorating our home. Liturgical seasons were celebrated, all as a matter of course. We went to a Catholic school. Regular Mass and reception of the sacraments were part of life. God was very much present in our lives, within and beyond our family.

Our family migrated to Australia in the early 1950s. After a period in migrant camps, we settled in Tulendeena, a beautiful valley in rural Tasmania. I have since learned that, long before it was named Tasmania, Aboriginal people knew the island as *lutruwita*. The land on which we settled was known as *tebrakunna* country to the *pairrebeener* people, the traditional 'owners' of North-East Tasmania.

Our new home had no running water, electricity or telephone. The property had been cleared of trees, but never cultivated. The land on which we tried to grow crops was covered with bracken fern and too hungry to bring forth a harvest. It took several years and much hard work to make it productive.

One day, not long after we came to Tulendeena, I was home from school to help Mum. I was washing the breakfast dishes on a bench behind our house when I heard voices behind me. Turning, I saw two women dressed in grey walking up the path. They were the Rosary House Sisters[1] At the time, my mother's English was very limited,

---

1 The Home Missionary Sisters of Our Lady, now known as Missionary Sisters of Service. At the time they were popularly named after the title of their homes, Rosary House.

and mine was a little better, but still quite limited. We managed to communicate over a cuppa. They were relaxed and at home with us, making us feel the same with them.

The Sisters came to our parish twice a year and always visited our home, and the homes of all the families of the parish. They took the children for religious instruction, prepared them for the sacraments and brought a lovely sense of welcome to our Sunday Mass. We were enrolled in their correspondence school of religious education, keeping alive our contact with them throughout the year. I looked forward to their regular visits. I left school the day I turned 15, as did all the older children in our family. The following week, we put a few vegetables from our garden on the old truck and my father and I went from door to door in the towns east of our valley. Over the following months and years we built up a regular round throughout the North-East district. We sold what we grew and supplemented our produce with that grown by other farmers and orchardists.

In my mid-teens, my priest-uncle, Piet Boonekamp CM, visited us. Each day he celebrated Mass in our living room. One day, listening to the Latin liturgy, watching him make signs of the cross over the bread and wine, something inside me shouted, 'Witchcraft! This is nothing but witchcraft'. With that, my faith and my world shattered: if the Mass wasn't what I believed it was, then what I had been taught about God wasn't true either? Then there was no basis to faith. More than that, there was no meaning or direction in life. This was crisis!

I desperately wanted there to be a God and – contradictory as it sounds – prayed to God that there be a God. But the inner darkness continued. There was no one I could confide in. I was ashamed, embarrassed: how could anyone possibly understand my 'faithlessness'? I don't know how long this inner darkness lasted. It seemed to me interminable. I continued to go to Mass, receive Communion and go to confession, join in our family prayers, not because I believed, but because I desperately wanted to believe.

Gradually, imperceptibly, the darkness began to lift. There was no particular experience by which to pinpoint the moment. As John O'Donoghue writes of the dawn: 'The first fingers of light appear on the horizon; ever so deftly and gradually, they pull the mantle of darkness away from the world'.[2] One day, I found myself in the dawning Light: I knew with my entire being that the faith I had grown up with was not only true, it was *Life*! With that, I fell in love with God, with Jesus, with the Church. In that in-loveness, I knew myself called to give myself totally to God in religious life.

But my deep desire was to be a mother, to have children of my own. For a time, I managed to ignore what I knew in my heart. But try as I might, there was a *Yes* in me I could not silence. Eventually, I told my mother what was in my heart. She replied, 'So that's what has been preoccupying you. Well, if that's what God wants...' I fled from the room and burst into tears – tears of relief (I had acknowledged the call) and tears of grief (I had relinquished my desire for children of my own). Shortly before my twentieth birthday, I joined the Missionary Sisters of Service.

---

2 John O'Donoghue, *Anam Cara: Spiritual Wisdom from the Celtic World*, Bantam Press 1997, p. 21.

Part II

Blossoming into a wider world

1
Beyond the garden gate

On 16 August 1959, my parents took me to Hobart in the vegetable truck, to the novitiate (formation house) of the Rosary House Sisters. We were warmly welcomed by Mother Teresa, the congregational leader, Sister Vianney, the novice mistress, and six novices. My parents stayed for afternoon tea, then set off for the long drive home. I couldn't hold back a few tears as I said goodbye to them and to the life I knew so well. At the same time, I felt a deep sense of peace in the Yes to the life I was about to begin.

Materially, our life was poor, but that was no hardship to me. It was no different from life at home. I loved our classes, held in the converted garage behind the main building. I was hungry for knowledge and understanding. Father John Wallis, the priest who founded the congregation in 1944, gave classes in theology, liturgy, spirituality and so on. There were daily periods for reading the Scriptures, other spiritual reading and times for meditation.

Early October that first year, our group of postulants (as we were called) made a three-day retreat, given by Father John. It was the first retreat I had ever made. That retreat opened me to a richness and beauty in our faith far beyond what I ever suspected. The image that came to me at the time was that my faith had been like a lovely, enclosed garden. I had no idea there was a world beyond this garden. But Father John opened the gate of that garden and showed us that world beyond. In the years since, I have not ceased exploring that world, not only as knowledge, but as experience and life.

I made my profession of vows in August 1962. I was ready (so I thought) to go into the highways and byways, like the sisters who had come to our parish so regularly. In reality I was far from ready. Our novitiate laid the foundations of theology and spirituality in us, and we had some basic teacher training, geared to religious education of children. But the practical aspects of our pastoral ministry were learned 'on the job'. We went out in pairs, the new ones with a sister a few years her senior. We noticed what helped and what didn't help.

There was no structure to this process of learning. We relied largely on intuition, though I wasn't conscious of this at the time.

My first posting was to Parkes in the Wilcannia-Forbes Diocese. Our mission took us throughout Western New South Wales, visiting people, gathering them for Mass and teaching their children. We stayed with them in their homes, or in church sacristies, Country Women's Association rooms or shearers' quarters on properties, whatever accommodation was available.

The people we lived and worked among were our greatest teachers in pastoral work. They invited us into their lives, entrusted us with their stories, their trials and tribulations, their friendship. I was amazed at how at ease I felt among them. Perhaps my family experience of the difficulties and challenges of life on the land, of isolation and loneliness, had given me an understanding and empathy for people as they experienced their own versions of such challenges. I loved that mission life.

Another profound formative influence on me was the country itself: the wide-open plains with their huge dome of sky, a land of drought and flood, of want and of plenty, depending on the seasons. Very few roads outside of the towns were sealed. The fine red dust settled into everything. In the summer, the scorching dry heat hardly cooled through the nights. During the day, sticky little flies crawled on our faces and backs. When rains came after a long dry spell, we witnessed an astounding transformation. Almost instantly, the red soil gained a covering of the greenest green and the land came alive. Water birds, sensing the elements, arrived in their multitudes. Fish would appear in dams and waterholes. Where did they come from? When the water dried up, they buried themselves deep in the Earth where moisture remains. When the waterholes filled again, they dug their way back to the surface. Nature is ever resilient in this big country and its sparse population of large-hearted people. Experiencing all this *did* something in me.

The silence and solitude of the plains met some deep, inarticulable space in my spirit. One day, we stopped the car. Walking some distance away from it, I stood still in that vast emptiness under that equally vast dome of sky. I felt utterly insignificant, yet totally embraced by the vastness that enveloped me. And on a moonless night, when the daytime blue of the sky gives way to the profound depths of night, the sky, now velvety black, is studded with billions of brilliant stars. The awe and mystery of the Universe spoke of God as totally beyond me, yet present in astounding intimacy.

In an imperceptible way, my experience of travelling in that country and being among its people enlarged me. It also enlarged my vision and understanding. Before the end of my first year in that Diocese, Mother Teresa and Father John visited us in Parkes. Sitting around the dining room table, sharing our experiences, I heard myself say things that surprised me: without my realising it, my small thinking had been broken open to perspectives I had not known earlier.

Looking back on those early years, I experience one serious regret. This is in regard to the Aboriginal people. We were so ignorant of their – and our – real history, of the destruction of their communities, their cultures and their languages, of children being forcibly removed from their parents, of the thousand and one ways in which government policies disregarded their rights, dignity and traditions, and justified its policies. The people, who inhabited this land since time immemorial, did not even have citizenship at the time, nor were they counted in the national census.

When we visited Aboriginal families, I felt a divide between them and us – a divide I did not know how to reach across. The adults seemed very shy and depressed. I had no idea that their depression was orchestrated by the White Australia Policy, by the way colonisers used and abused them, and presumed they had a right to assume sovereignty over a sovereign people! The truth is that the colonisers were intruders who wanted Aboriginal labour but did not pay them wages, who removed them from *Country*, suppressed their languages and culture, and killed them when they fought back. It was as though the original inhabitants of this land had no right even to exist. And I did not know! I find it hard to comprehend how I could have not known.

Towards the end of January 1965, after two and a half years in the Wilcannia-Forbes Diocese, I was appointed to Ellendale in Tasmania. Ellendale was a mission centre taking in the upper Derwent Valley, reaching into the highlands at the southern end of the Lakes country which birthed the Derwent River. Instead of periodic visits to parishes, two of us were in the area throughout the year. Each week we visited ten schools in ten different towns spread over some 20,000 square miles, taking the children for their weekly religious instruction. In between and after classes, we visited their families.

On Sundays, we went to three different towns for Mass. There were four branches of the Catholic Women's League in the area and we attended their monthly meetings. Our lives in that upper Derwent Valley were crazily busy and challenging, but we were young, full of energy and enthusiasm. I loved it. Half a century has gone by since I was there, but I still remember those years and many of the people with deep affection.

During these years, the liturgical changes instigated by the Second Vatican Council were beginning to be implemented. The renewed appreciation of the Church as the People of God, a community in which everyone is a participant, found expression in the liturgy. We introduced people to the renewed liturgy and the reasons for the changes.

The teachings of Vatican II made their impact on our own lives too. They brought a new freedom, together with a new level of responsibility in the way our MSS community, and I personally, lived and responded to the Gospel.

In 1971, inspired by the vision of Vatican II, we adopted a new name for our congregation, Missionary Sisters of Service, a title that continually reminds us that our mission is to serve in the spirit of Jesus. More than fifty years later, that title continues to call me to serve in love. Service has become a quality of spirituality, colouring who I am and whatever I do.

2
A life-changing experience

All my life, I have been hungry to learn. Throughout the years of the sixties and seventies, I enrolled in various correspondence courses, in education, in scripture, theology, and so on. It wasn't so much about learning for its own sake, but so that I might have a deeper understanding and context for my own life and be better equipped for the mission in which I was engaged.

In 1971, I was offered the opportunity to do a course in catechetical and pastoral renewal at the East Asian Pastoral Institute in Manila, Philippines. I was one of eighty-four participants that year, coming from over thirty countries. All of us were engaged in the pastoral mission of the Church, many in countries other than their own.

Most of the lecturers had themselves spent years on mission among people of cultures different from their own. They understood the challenges facing those who worked in such situations. The course was designed to equip us more adequately for our mission. Besides theology and catechetics, it included units in psychology, Islam, Hinduism and Buddhism, on culture and acculturation. It sowed the first seeds of what in later years became my interest in inter-faith groups and in the wisdom within other faith traditions.

I made many friends among my fellow students and for years afterwards kept up correspondence with a number of them. I also fell in love with one of the men. That was a beautiful and painful experience: beautiful, in that it awoke in me a depth of affectivity I had not known; painful, in that it ignited my sexual longings and the yearning for a life-companion which I knew could not be fulfilled. Sensing Frank's vulnerability, I also felt responsible for safeguarding him in his vocation.

Over the next year or so, I felt I was living with a divided heart, longing to be with Frank and desiring to be faithful to the Yes which Christ had implanted in me and that persisted even while the other desire tugged at my heart so powerfully.

Looking back on that time, I am deeply grateful for the experience. It enriched and matured me. The experience of falling in love cracked open my heart and released capacities for love, warmth and affection I had not known in myself, qualities which endured long after the emotional turmoil resolved itself.

The Philippines also gave me an experience of the divide between rich and poor. The wealthy seemed to flaunt their wealth ostentatiously, with large, flash houses in gated and guarded neighbourhoods, employing the poor to serve them, often with little acknowledgment or gratitude, and for pitifully small wages.

Travelling in Manila in a jeepney or bus was an experience of immersion in humanity. I vividly remember being on a crowded old bus inching its way across an intersection with a small side street. As I looked up that small street, I saw one moving mass of people. In that moment, I was struck by the realisation that God knew each of those people as intimately as I believed God knew me! Of course, I had always known that God knew and loved every person. In this moment, the enormity of that reality came home to me with amazing immediacy.

Upon returning to Tasmania, I was asked to prepare new courses for our correspondence schools in religious education. I took up this new assignment with zest, eager to put my new learnings to use. Besides preparing lessons for children, I prepared a small book of short reflections for their parents, to help them understand the approach to the lessons and the thinking behind them. I delighted in sharing with parents something of what I had received that had so enlivened me.

In 1973, I was posted back to Parkes NSW, the Diocese of my first mission experience. I was delighted to return to the places and people I had come to love ten years earlier. This time, my main focus was on training people as catechists so they could go into the schools for the weekly religion period, or conduct Sunday school classes. I loved that work. I came to realise that my natural *forte* was working with adults, and particularly in education. I felt myself expand in the work, learning as much from the people I taught as they learned from me.

After two very satisfying years in Wilcannia-Forbes Diocese, I was unexpectedly asked to come back to Tasmania, to Lindisfarne, Hobart. This move took me into a whole new chapter of my life.

3
The revealing power of words

My assignment to our mother house (as it was then called) in Lindisfarne brought a sudden halt to the direction I had envisaged I would travel for the years of my active life. My passion and energy were for the mission among the people on the highways and byways of rural and outback Australia. Now, after thirteen years in various places, I was asked to do my outreach from a desk. But the *Yes* within me would not let me refuse.

I was appointed leader of the community which included the congregational leader. I often felt caught between her expectations and those of the community. I tried to be all things to all of them (cf. 1 Corinthians 9:22) – an impossible ideal. Father John frequently quoted to us a Latin saying, *humano modo*, in a human way. I still had much to learn about living my life and carrying out my responsibilities *humano modo*. Meanwhile, it caused me much stress.

One day, when things seemed wrong on many scores, on impulse I took pen to paper and wrote furiously all that was 'wrong'. As I wrote, I also started to name what I was feeling about these matters. When I had vented it all, I read over my scribble. Wow! It was as though a lightbulb went on: suddenly, I saw what was going on in me! I had found the key to access to my inner self, the self I sensed was there but I had not been able to reach. It was May 1977. From then on, I kept a journal. It became my confidante, a mirror in which I came to know myself.

Writing has made me aware of the extraordinary power of words. I never cease to wonder at the capacity we humans have to communicate our thoughts, ideas, questions and imaginings to another. We translate what is in our minds into sounds, words. Choosing the right 'sounds', I can convey to another what I wish to share with them. They do so in return. Words can inform, encourage, create, evoke, hurt, heal, build up, destroy, deceive, betray, invite, lift hearts, cast them down and much, much more. That is their amazing power!

Much of my work at the time required writing: preparing correspondence courses for families, writing articles, and editing our congregational newsletter, *Highways and Byways*. I put together my first issue of the latter, pleased with what I had done. The congregational leader read it and asked me to show it Father John. From the moment he read the first sentence, he started to pull it to pieces. I was devastated: he had not even read the whole paragraph, let alone the article!

So began my apprenticeship in writing, learning to construct sentences, paragraphs and stories. It was a painful process. I had not realised the poverty of my skills in English and my lack of understanding of its structure and grammar. Over the next year or so, Father John taught me the finer skills of good writing. Because I identified so closely with what I wrote, these lessons cost me many tears. But their gift was invaluable. In the years since, I have drawn constantly on the skills he honed so patiently in me.

The initial idea of writing my story came from a desire to plot the journey of my inner life. I looked to my journals to help me remember. I was unprepared for what I found there. My journals introduced me to the woman I was some forty years earlier, meeting her at a level of intimacy that was almost overwhelming. The colours and textures of those years had slipped from my memory. But they are all there, in my journals.

The woman of my thirties and forties was intense, often anxious, feeling she didn't quite belong. A sense of loneliness and alienation pervaded her, despite being part of, and fully involved in, community. Her anxiety was intensified in her inability to pray. She was afraid of drifting from God. She sometimes wondered whether she really had any faith. The growing competence of her outer life was in stark contrast to her sense of inadequacy in her inner life. It caused her great anguish. She wrote:

> *What is the swirling force that has hold of me, that draws from me a yearning like the thirst of drought-stricken land, like the hunger of starvation, bitter-sweet with sadness and joy? How often this force takes hold of me with the violence of passion fully aroused, and with the sense of*

> *hope that you will break the shackles that bind me and set me free to follow where you lead. At the same time, a sense of despair, that I will ever enter that intimacy with you for which my whole being longs.*   4.7.1977

And yet, there were moments of grace that came as refreshing blessings, like rain on parched land. One day, I was walking along the water's edge at Penna, Tasmania. As I rounded the rocks of Shark Point, I paused where the bay opened before me, the hills of Richmond in the background. I experienced something which even now I find difficult to describe. It was as though my eyes were opened to see the scene before me in a new dimension. There was something extraordinarily clear and immediate about it. I felt addressed by it through every faculty of perception. It lasted just a few moments. Then my vision returned to normal. As I walked back around the rocky point, I found myself singing,

> *Dance in the darkness, slow be the pace.*
> *Surrender to the rhythm of redeeming grace.*[3]

Towards the end of my first journal, I look back over the months and begin to see an emerging theme:

> *Today the final scene of my June retreat came back to me, with the invitation to let go all I am and all I know, in order that the Lord might show me who he really is and that he might make me what he really intends me to become. And the further invitation: to go to the ends of the earth with him without him. It all adds up to one thing: Leave self behind and come with me.*   7.2.1978

---

3 Carey Landry, from the album *Abba Father*, North American Liturgy Resources – SE-17, North American Liturgy Resources – ABBA-LAN-CS.

4
. . . And her name is Corrie

Who – or what – am I? This was the underlying question of my life during my thirties and forties. From childhood I had a belief that, if I was to grow in intimacy with God, I needed to make myself acceptable to God. Gospel sayings such as, 'Be perfect as your heavenly Father is perfect' (Matthew 5:48), were firmly lodged in my consciousness.

My understanding of perfection was an impossible ideal. It took no account of my human frailty and did not allow for failures – and I experienced plenty of both. I had not connected my demand for perfection to *humano modo*.

The more I came to know myself, the more I became aware of my lack of perfection, my sinfulness. There are many entries that mention feeling envious, jealous, angry, self-centred, cowardly, defensive, judgmental, needy for approval, and so on. As I came to recognise and name what was going on within me, I was able to confide something of it to others. I regularly comment on the comfort I found when I could lay bare my inner life to another (often Father John) and be heard and understood. I expressed this in a brief poem:

> *The peace that comes*
> *from being known,*
> *understood,*
> *accepted in weakness,*
> *baseness,*
> *pettiness.*
> *It makes me feel*
> *washed clean inside.*

My journals of these years are dotted with entries such as, *Corrie, you need to let go the Corrie you think you ought to be, so that you can become the Corrie I made you to be.* It took me years to get this. I looked outside myself, to others, for clues to knowing who or what I ought to be. To be acceptable seemed of critical importance for my sense of self and of belonging. The longing to belong, to be someone for someone, was like a hidden wound within me.

Reflecting today on the recurring issue of feeling unacceptable, I suspect my basic problem was not so much that I was unacceptable to others, but that I had not accepted myself as I was. I had not yet learnt to become compassionate towards myself as God was compassionate towards me. I was part of a community of women who truly loved one another. Yet I doubted my lovableness.

There is another invitation that appears from time to time in my journals: *Corrie, you have to let go of the Jesus you think you know so that he may show you the Jesus he is*. It parallels the saying of letting go of the Corrie I think I am or ought to be. There was much more to the meek and mild Jesus I learnt about as a child. Over the years, the experience of suffering led me to a more robust Jesus – one who laid down his life for the life of the world; one who loved even unto death. But at that stage of my life, I could hardly name my pain as suffering, let alone see it in the context of Jesus' crucifixion. Compared with his, my suffering seemed too insignificant to claim anything as lofty as laying down my life.

Mid 1978, I made an eight-day retreat at John Fisher College, Hobart. The college nestles in the foothills of Mount Nelson with natural bush covering its flanks. Each day, I walked the track to the top of the hill, delighting in the rich beauty and diversity of the bush. There, I found a place of stillness, silence. I experienced a peace in simply being there. On one of those walks I was reciting, without realising I was doing so, the first chapter of John's Gospel:

> *In the beginning was the word and the word was with God and the word was God... And the word was made flesh and* **her name was Corrie**.

That last phrase jolted me out of my reverie. I felt confused, embarrassed, ashamed: how dare I assume to myself the reality that belonged to Jesus, the Word incarnate! It seemed sacrilegious. When I mentioned it to my retreat director, he passed over it and sent me to another passage of the Scriptures, unconnected with this experience. But I could not move on so easily. The phrase continued to reverberate in me. Perhaps it *did* come from the Spirit.

As I continued to mull over this experience, the opening chapter of the book of Genesis came to mind, the creation story, in which every word God spoke became what that word indicated: it became light, dry land and seas, trees, animals and human beings. Was the phrase that so shocked me, actually telling me something deeper about myself than I had heretofore realised? Could it be that the entire creation, in some mysterious way, is an incarnation? Is there a sense in which I am an incarnation of the Word? The more I reflected on this question, the more I sensed its truth. As far as I knew, I had never heard anything like this taught anywhere. If what I heard that day was true, then the Christian tradition I grew up in had hardly begun to unpack the mystery of incarnation, the Word made flesh.

That was more than forty years ago. And, as has happened on other occasions, when some significant new insight comes to me, after a while I hear of other people who are working on that same insight. Over the years, I encountered books and articles exploring this core mystery of our Christian faith, and its implications for how we understand ourselves, creation and our place in the Cosmos. Such understanding has profound implications for how we relate to one another and to every part of creation. As I grew into that realisation, I began to read the scriptures with new understanding.

The Word was made flesh and her name is Corrie. Yes. And her name is each of the women of my community. Every man, woman and child ever born is a Word of God made flesh, including those we find hard to love. And the mystery is not only in human beings. Every creature, every part of creation, planets, stars and galaxies, everything that exists is God's self-expression, each reflecting some unique facet of God's unfathomable mystery. At the deepest level of our being and our identity is the mystery of God, the indwelling Trinity.

This is getting ahead of my story. I did not see all that in 1978. But the experience during that walk up the Mount Nelson track held the core of something that, over the years, with reflection on the experiences of daily life, the writings of mystics, theologians, poets and scientists, gradually revealed itself as the foundational reality of all that exists, the Christ mystery. It was as though God said,

> *Corrie, you worry about your identity, recognition? I'll show you who you are. The Word was made flesh and her name is Corrie! That is your real identity. And remember,*

you share that identity with every other being of the Cosmos. That's where you are accepted, where you belong, a precious infinitesimal part of my precious creation.

Many years would pass before I could hear this truth for what it really is.

5
The extraordinary ordinary

Love and gratitude: these two themes pervade my journals. Again and again, no matter the context of the moment, I express my gratitude. Over the years, gratitude has become the dominant melody of my life. I believe that gratitude is the root of the deep inner joy I have always experienced, even in the midst of difficult, confusing or painful situations. My sense of gratitude has grown as I have become more aware of the giftedness of life and all it holds. My journals also record a growing appreciation of grace and beauty as I encounter these in various situations.

As I write 'grace and beauty', I am taken back to the 1980s, watching Jane Torvill and Christopher Dean performing their ice-dancing to the music of Bolero. Their dancing lifted me into a realm of sheer transcendent delight. But moments of grace and beauty need not be that spectacular. There is a grace and beauty in the ordinary everyday. Over the years, I have grown to love and appreciate the ordinary. The ordinary is the rhythm of day and night, marked by sunset and sunrise. It is the air we breathe, the coordination of eye, hands and feet that enables us to drive a vehicle, jump puddles and manipulate complex things. Almost all the elements that make up our daily lives – relationships, work, leisure, community, and prayer – are ordinary... until we really see them for what they are.

When I am truly present to what is in my immediate surroundings, I find myself surprised by the simple things in life: the flash of colour of the rainbow lorikeet alighting on the grevillea at my elbow as I walk by; the spontaneous delight on the child's face as she watches the bubbles she has blown float through the air; a new shoot on a plant I thought was dying; the shine of the kitchen floor after it has been washed; a note of support left under my door or a shared experience of silent wonder; it can be the look between young lovers, or a glass of fresh water on a hot day, or the sparkle of sunlight on the bird-bath...

Even extraordinary moments of life are grounded in the ordinary. We need the ordinary everyday to integrate what we are experiencing, enabling us to grow, like the seed in the ground, without our being aware while it is happening. The ordinary is continually creating me into who and what I am becoming. It is truly extraordinary! The rare special moments, when I glimpse something that lifts me into sharper awareness, are invitations to me to wake up to the gift of the ordinary in every moment of every day.

It took me many years to appreciate the gift of the ordinary, including the ordinariness of myself. I carried a hidden ambition to be extraordinary, to make an impact on the world, to be a saint, all the time lacked the courage to stand out from the ordinary. Besides, I was aware that the Gospel tells us to seek the lowest place. But lack of courage is not humility. In my earlier years, I didn't understand that true humility begins with accepting the truth of myself, as I am, in this moment, neither more nor less.

In fact, I was afraid of knowing the full truth of myself, lest it was even worse than I feared. And what if, when I came to see my deeper self, I were to find nothing there? I was terrified of the deep emptiness I often felt within myself.

While sitting at prayer during my retreat in 1979, I heard an invitation: 'Give me yourself and I will show you yourself'. With that I froze. I simply couldn't do it. My fear paralysed me. I pleaded with the Lord, 'I can't. Just take me'. But no, he could only take me if the gift came from me. I sat there, immobilised, for perhaps an hour. Then, quietly, subtly, something changed. My fear melted away like morning mist in the rising sun. I handed myself over and watched as Jesus took me and held me in his hands as though I were a ball. He held that ball that was me with infinite tenderness. And that was it! I saw then that it was my fears that prevented me from living fully. I didn't need courage to realise my ambitions; I needed courage to be and to live as the woman I am, the courage to be human.

As I continued to prepare material for our correspondence courses in religious education, I kept pondering: How can I write about God and the teachings that lie at the heart of the Gospel in a way that might touch the hearts and lives of the children and their parents? How can I write in a way that can lead them to experience something of the amazing mystery of God?

I needed to find words and images for my own experience of God, of Jesus, and for the depth of meaning and relationship that was central to my life. During these years, I pondered deeply what I knew in my heart yet found impossible to convey in words. In my journal, I wrote:

> *I see myself as living on the fringe of a vast spiritual reality – it is there, in my consciousness, yet eludes my consciousness. It is as though I am veiled. I long to tear away the veil to see. But only God can lift it. And if God does – can I enter that World and live?*   20.5.1979

I wasn't the only teacher struggling with such questions. At that time, religious education of children was undergoing re-evaluation all over the English-speaking world. Earlier approaches were not working as they should. The social contexts of family life and society were changing drastically. The faith community in which I was born and raised was no more. But what that community was to become in our rapidly changing universe was beyond our knowing. We were in unknown territory and hardly realised it.

Part III

Journey through chaos

1
Disintegration

My six years at Lindisfarne came to an end with our Chapter of January 1981. The Chapter is a time when, as a congregation, we review our life and mission. It is a process of listening to the wisdom of our lived experience and what is happening in our world in the light of the Gospel and re-set our mission focus accordingly. In the months leading up to this event, I had been heavily involved in the preparations for this six-yearly gathering of the congregation.

During that Chapter, a dam burst within me. I had just finished facilitating a session when suddenly and unexpectedly I burst into tears. I cried and cried and couldn't stop, though I didn't know why I was crying. It seemed like all the stresses and tensions of the previous weeks and months and years had come to a head. I was at a junction which catapulted me into a period of profound brokenness. Some weeks later, I wrote:

> *Chapter is behind us – yet it shows promise of being with me for a long time yet. I have not yet had time to distance myself from it in order to find a perspective. The weeks leading up to Chapter and the time of Chapter itself were intensely concentrated. My mind was constantly stretched, trying to hear, and express in writing what I heard, searching out its implications, and keeping an eye on the numerous facets of Chapter. I was very aware of you at work in the deeper reaches of myself, stripping me day by day of my self-centred ambitions and desires. Cecilia[4] called it a Chapter of tears, and it was that for me.*
> 2.2.1981

The experience left me in a state of spiritual disintegration, or so it felt at the time. I was appointed to Launceston and to the parish missions in rural Tasmania. For the previous six years I had

---

4 Cecilia Bailey mss, who was elected leader at that Chapter.

yearned to be back in that work. Now the pain of leaving Lindisfarne overwhelmed me. It seems paradoxical that the place that had brought me so much grief, I now found so hard to leave. Kahlil Gibran's words resonated with me:

> How shall I go in peace and without sorrow?
> Nay, not without a wound in the spirit shall I leave this city.
> Long were the days of pain I have spent within its walls,
> And long were the nights of aloneness.
> And who can depart from his place of aloneness without regret?

Yet I knew it was imperative that I go:

> For to stay, though the hours burn in the night,
> Is to freeze and crystallise and be bound in a mould.[5]
>
> 11.2.1981

I went to Launceston feeling desolate. For the following two years, I was involved in the pastoral mission among people in rural Tasmania. But I struggled. It seemed that all my competencies had turned to dust and ashes. I felt an abysmal failure. In the sacrament of reconciliation, I spoke about myself as a broken vessel. Very gently, the priest, Tony O'Brien msc, cupped his hands and said, 'When our container breaks, God cups his hands around the shards so that nothing may be lost'. This consoling image sustained me through much of that painful time.

Despite my inner chaos and brokenness, I managed a degree of functioning in my outer life. I felt more vulnerable than I had ever experienced. Yet I had an inkling that this experience was necessary for my growth. I turned to various authors, trying to come to some understanding of what was going on within me. I felt the Lord was calling me to deeper self-surrender, but I found myself resisting. My ego struggled desperately to stay in control.

I felt unable to pray and I was afraid of drifting, of going astray on this desert journey. One day, reflecting on the calming of the storm

---

5 Kahlil Gibran, *The Prophet*, William Heineman Ltd, London 1971. pp. 1-2.

(Matthew 8:23-27), I noted Jesus' chiding his disciples: 'O ye of little faith, why did you doubt?' He was chiding me: Why do I doubt in this stormy night of my life? Then it struck me:

> *How could you let me stray? What kind of God do I believe in? You love me infinitely more than I can ever love myself or anyone else. Would you let me stray? A gentle confidence slipped into me.* 30.6.1981

I was reminded of the invitation that came to me in an earlier retreat:

> *Will you go to the ends of the Earth with me without me? Much of my life has been precisely that – with you without you, coming to know you in the darkness of not knowing, recognising your presence in absence.* 23.5.1981

Throughout this time of brokenness, I was aware of a bottomless need to be loved and cared for by another – or others. But I also became aware that, if I were to give my neediness free rein, I would drain those who were supportive of me. While I needed their support, I could not – must not – use them to fill my need. That need, too, had to be surrendered.

Today, I recognise a deeper necessity for such restraint. The experience of brokenness, weakness and vulnerability was essential to my maturing into the person I am created to be. There is an inner child in me who wants mummy to kiss her better, to fix whatever is causing my pain. But as an adult, I need to take responsibility for my life in all its ups and downs. I need to enter as fully into my experience of painful emptiness as I do in experiences of abundance and creative vitality. All the support in the world cannot live the journey for me. I must walk it alone, and experience deeply the aloneness of it. It is the only way to learn to live in my own skin, to become my own person.

Reflecting on that time in my life, I am taken to the agony in the garden (Matthew 26:36-44). Jesus asked his disciples to wait and pray while he walked on alone. In his aloneness, the full import of what he was facing overwhelmed him. He was terrified and prayed that the cup of suffering might pass him by. He went back to his disciples, seeking their support, but they had fallen asleep. So again, he walked alone...

Without over dramatising my experience, I too prayed in agony to be relieved of the pain and brokenness that had overtaken me. At the same time, my journal records my realisation that this painful phase of my life was essential to my growth. My prayer that God, who seemed to be so absent, would draw near and relieve me of the pain, was often followed by a plea that it not be relieved until its purpose was achieved in me.

As I reflect on those years of disintegration and of gradually being rebuilt, I recognise that this was the midlife crisis that psychology identifies as a significant stage of life. During early adult years, our focus is predominantly on the outer world, on developing competencies to function well in that world. Then there comes a time when life begins to stir in its deeper dimension. It confronts us with questions such as, Who am I really? What is the meaning and purpose of my life? Where and to whom do I really belong? Such questions precipitate an inner crisis. The anchorage points of our earlier life no longer hold, and we find ourselves adrift in unknown territory.

2
Journey through chaos

> Gnarled trunk
> carved and sculpted
> by the elements:
> harsh westerlies have hurt you;
> frosts and snows have toughened you.
> Life's experience has given you
> a beauty all your own.
> Rich the colours of your coat,
> yet it has served your need.
> Soon it will be doffed
> and be replaced by one
> not yet painted by wind and weather
> into the rich warmth of age
> Is this the story of a tree?
> Or a parable?

The photo that gave rise to this poem is pasted on the cover of one of my journals. It is much faded by now. Yet still, contemplating it, together with the poem, I am struck by its beauty and the hopeful wisdom it held for my midlife years. Already in the early 1980s I caught a glimpse of this wisdom.

Towards the end of 1982, I moved to Melbourne. This opened new opportunities for me as I continued to muddle through the middle years of my life. I sought counselling and availed myself of regular spiritual direction. Both greatly aided my growing self-awareness, discovering issues I needed to address and inner strengths I could draw on.

I enrolled in part-time study at Yarra Theological Union, meeting my hunger to deepen my understanding of the faith in which I had been nurtured since birth. A passage in John's Gospel became my mantra during those years:

> If you make my word your home,
> you will indeed be my disciples,
> you will learn the truth
> and the truth will set you free. (John 8:31-32)

In my journal I note: *The search for truth is an awesome responsibility.* I longed for truth, and I longed to be free. But the truth I needed to know has many layers. One of these is the truth of myself – all of it, the good, the bad and the indifferent, unadorned by excuses.

During those difficult years, my 'negatives' seemed to face me at every turn. Gradually, as I learned to accept myself as I am, I became gentler, more compassionate towards myself, and also with others. At the same time, I came to appreciate the giftedness of my life, to let go the need to bring a judgment of good, bad, or indifferent. I am not compartmentalised into what is acceptable and unacceptable: God loves me as I am, the whole of me. This is something I've had to learn again and again.

I had grown up accepting that Church was the custodian of the truth of the Gospel. While that is so, that custody is exercised by very human instruments and laws, conditioned by the history and cultures of the people who formulated them. The living truth cannot be confined in formulae and accepted orthodoxies. When we attempt to do so, truth becomes fossilised and can no longer give us life. The truth Jesus spoke of calls us beyond doctrine and teachings. It calls us to intimacy with him. He is the truth that sets us free (cf. John 15). He frequently chides scribes and pharisees for their insistence on the exact precepts of the law:

> *Their goodness did not set them free – it enslaved them. You have come to set me free. I too am often bound by the book, by people's expectations (real or imagined) of me... Yet, side by side with your freedom from the law, there is an imperative much more demanding: the Father's love, the Father's mission. This is not as easy as following the rules. It involves the heat and pain of passion, the cold and darkness of death, of failure, of seeing your life's work collapse, of surrender in naked faith...* 26.5.1981

To make our home in his Word is to make our home in Jesus as he is in the Father. And conversely, the Father and the Son make their home in us. This is intimacy indeed, a relationship of mutual love and mutual indwelling.

In earlier years, I was comfortable in the security and certainty offered by laws, rules and authorities. But my growing understanding demanded a deeper responsibility – response–ability. This the real meaning of my vow of obedience. It is obedience to the truth which sets us free, the truth which is Christ. I find it an awesome responsibility!

Another theme that runs through my journals during these years relates to poverty. 'Blessed are the poor in spirit', said Jesus in the sermon on the mount (Matthew 5:3). This poverty is not about what we have or don't have. It is a spiritual quality, an inner freedom in relation to material things and status, to be as ready to give as to receive, to be grateful for what every moment holds; to be generous in all dimensions of my life.

During the mid-years of my life, coming face to face with my own brokenness brought me to realise a poverty that is deeper than all other forms of poverty. It is the innate condition of my being. As I faced my inability to heal myself, to bring about change or conversion in myself, to let go the securities I cling to, to overcome my resistance, and so on, I became aware of my utter inner poverty, and with it, of my utter dependence on God. I wrote in my Journal:

> (The course on prayer and spirituality) *helped me to explore more deeply my experience of inner poverty, my powerlessness and sinfulness. In earlier years, I experienced a call to a deeper expression of poverty in my use of material goods, in my willingness to be available, to give of myself, my time and energy. But all the time there was power in that way of living out my vision of poverty. I could choose to do otherwise than I did. I was in charge. That kind of poverty was an option I could, but need not, choose.*
>
> *The inner poverty the Lord has revealed to me is no option. It is a radical being what I am. I cannot run away from it. If I deny or ignore it, it is still what I am in the*

> *ultimate reality of my being. The experience is filled with paradox: it has been filled with pain, with brokenness, with a sense of lostness and utter helplessness. At the same time, it has released in me a new capacity to love, to reach out compassionately, to accept and understand both myself and others. This has been a discovery of riches – not riches that give me power, but riches that enable me to rejoice and to find strength and resolve to enter more fully into my condition as the Lord reveals it.*   6.8.1984

In earlier years, I was terrified of knowing my deeper self, lest, when I entered my deeper interior – I found nothing there. Now I knew it was true, there is nothing within me that I can claim as me or mine. All is grace, poured out on me by a gracious God who is rich in mercy and full of compassion (Psalm 145). 'What have you that you have not received?' asks St. Paul (1 Corinthians 4:7). This recognition brings about a deeper humility. I have enjoyed so many gifts, talents and achievements over the years. My ego-self gloried in them. But at root, it was all God's doing: 'Without me you can do nothing' (John 15:5).

In the course on Prayer and Christian Spirituality, Brian Gallagher msc often gave us questions to reflect on. All of them related to experiences I had journaled about. I found the group's sharing of those experiences enormously affirming. The matters I struggled with were also those that others experienced; they are part of who we are as human beings. Each one's experience is uniquely theirs; yet there is a commonality which I recognised in the sharing. What I had felt as failure or inadequacy in my life was actually part and parcel of the journey of growth and development as a human being. I can relate to God only as I am and at the stage of growth at which I am. This course was a real grace for me at this stage of my life.

The realisation of my innate poverty gave rise to the prayer of adoration. I suspect that at root, adoration is the recognition that there is nothing I can give God that God has not first given me. In that recognition, I can only bow down in humble, grateful and loving adoration. A passage in the book of Revelation gave me an image of this prayer:

> Every time... the twenty-four elders prostrated themselves before him
> to worship the One who lives for ever and ever,
> and threw down their crowns in front of the throne.
> (Revelation 4:9-10)

Every time! That arrested my attention: the elders would have had to pick up their crowns again before they could throw them down again. Then it dawned on me that this is what I do when I adore: again and again I bring all I am and have – i.e. my nothingness and emptiness – before God. I have nothing else to bring. But, like the twenty-four elders, I take myself back again and again.

Adoration is the prayer of utter poverty. At the same time, it is an experience of the incomprehensible richness of God's abundant self-giving to us and to all creation.

Adoration became the focus of my retreat that year:

> *(Prayer) is not just praise and thanks which focus on what you have given and done for us, but also adoration in which I can only come before you utterly empty of anything I might give, but pouring out my poverty, my emptiness in recognition of your holiness... Maybe that, too, is what your life was all about, poured out in adoration of the Father:*
>
>> *He did not cling to his equality with God,*
>> *but emptied himself...*
>> *and being as all humans are, he was humbler yet,*
>> *even to accepting death, death on a cross...* (Philippians 2:6-8)
>
> *It seems strange, but somehow adoration is linked to the mystery of death, even while it is life.... In a sense, in adoration we return all to you, leaving nothing for ourselves – and that is a kind of dying.*   23.8.1984

In adoration, my focus is totally on God:

> *It is easy to fall into the trap of relating everything to ourselves, with ourselves as the focus. Tonight, I felt that*

the focus should be on you, that my own healing and needs should be 'forgotten' as you reveal yourself as the Holy One. Like you said in the Gospel, 'The poor you will always have with you', so I will always be in need of you. But can I focus on you in silent worship? Can I focus on being present to your holiness – for your sake? Whatever adoration I offer you, I can only give because you have so gifted me in the first place. But is it not important for me to return to you for your sake, to return, not just thanks and praise which focus on what you have given and done for us, but also adoration in which I can only come before you utterly empty of anything I might give, pouring out my poverty, my emptiness, in recognition of your holiness?
23.8.1984

On the last day of that retreat, I wrote:

Tonight, as I reflected on my time with you, I realised that there have been no highs, no experiences of felt intimacy, nothing sensible of sweetness or suffering. The hours of prayer often seemed long and dry. Yet you have revealed yourself to me at a deeper level of my being, in the obscurity of faith, where only on looking back I can recognise where you have been, what you have touched in me, what you have revealed to me. This is the tenor of my everyday life and prayer. 27.8.1984

Reading through my journal, I am amazed at the richness that arises out of the 'nothing' that I am. I recognise this only when I listen deeply to what arises from my heart. In my case, the key to such listening is journaling.

3
With no other light

One very windy day, I was travelling on a bus along Port Philip Bay. I was reading Mark's Gospel and came to the passage about the disciples caught in a storm on the lake. Their boat was taking on water. They were terrified, and Jesus was asleep. The disciples woke him: 'Master, don't you care! We are going down!' Looking at the stormy bay with its white capped waves, I could sympathise with their predicament. Jesus calmed the storm, turned to them and said, 'Why are you so frightened? How is it that you have no faith?' (Mark 4:35-41). Spontaneously, I challenged the Lord: 'How can they *not* be afraid in that storm when you are asleep?' It was as much an accusation as a question. The fact was, I was in the midst of a storm and Jesus was asleep in my boat – or was he there at all?

Many journal entries of the late '70s and early '80s express my concern at an absence of faith. I have no sense of God. I am unable to pray. I feel lost, without a sense of direction. I had read about the dark night of John of the Cross and other spiritual writers. Was this some sort of dark night? Had it really felt dark, I might have recognised it. But I seemed to be in a dense mist, nothing like anything I had heard or read about.

I knew the theory of the necessity of times of loss and absence in the spiritual journey, but I could not recognise my experience in what the spiritual masters described. That not-knowing was itself part of the darkness. I needed to be stripped of all self-seeking in order to come to that deeper union with God that I longed for. What I know now is that this union was already a reality in me. God longs for me infinitely more than I long for God. I just did not know it at the time. I confused the consolation of God with the God of consolation.

Despite the pain of this period of my life, I also knew a deep-down sense of peace. I was like Peter, walking on water, afraid I would drown (Matthew 14:28-33). At the same time, I knew a security in the depth of my insecurity. Also, I knew joy even in the midst of pain and anxiety:

As I was going up the stairs at YTU today, I saw Kim in the stream of students going down and greeted her. When she saw me a few minutes later, she said, 'Corrie, you have such a beautiful smile when you greet me. It says something about a great joy within you'. I was surprised. How can that be, when I experience myself so broken, so confused, so messy? Yet, as I looked within myself, I knew Kim was right. There is a special kind of joy in me, side by side with, or in the midst of, all the things that are going on in me. What a precious gift that is. Thank you, Lord, thank you.
12.6.1984

Over the years, I have come to understand that joy is the other side of suffering. The Vietnamese Buddhist monk, Thich Nhat Hanh, says suffering and happiness *inter-are*. They exist together. Suffering is the mud out of which the lotus of love can grow.[6] That reflects my experience. My hunger and thirst for God were nurturing and purifying my love for God. It also deepened my love and compassion for people. There is deep joy in that love, and it can grow and deepen only through suffering. Suffering is the process of letting go of myself so that the love of God, the God of Love, can have full rein/reign in me: 'The love of God has been poured into our hearts by the Holy Spirit who dwells in us' (Romans 5:5). This is the paschal mystery that is the core of our Christian faith.

Today, I know that the dark night never comes to an end in this life. But, as I learn to surrender to it, my relationship with it changes. I think it was Thomas Green sj, commenting on the dark night of John of the Cross, who wrote, 'If we remain in the darkness long enough, it becomes itself a kind of light'.[7]

During those years, there were moments – rare but very real – when something crept through the fog. One such experience was at Easter 1983. I have always loved the liturgies of Holy Week and the Easter Vigil. That year I could not enter into the spirit of those events:

---

6 https://www.youtube.com/watch?v=NJ9UtuWfs3U
7 I can't locate the quote, but it comes from one of several books on prayer he published in the 1980s. I read them all and found much encouraging wisdom in them.

I felt like an impassive bystander, and wondered, where is my faith? I went to the 9.00 a.m. Eucharist again on Easter Sunday morning. When we came to the renewal of our baptismal commitment, I knew again with extraordinary certainty that my faith is real, no matter how devoid of any feeling, that without faith my life would be utter black despair... Tears ran down my face: I was filled with gratitude at the assurance that faith in me is real.
5.4.1983

Despite the assurance that came to me in that moment, I still felt empty and bereft. Tears continued to run down my face as I walked home. Then, as I came to Blackburn Lake, I sensed that my heart was being held. It was so subtle, I could easily have missed it. It wasn't something I felt; I just knew it in some dark way. Once I registered it, I could not doubt its reality. I also knew I had been held all along, and guided through the darkness:

> ... with no other light or guide
> than the one that burned in my heart;
> This guided me
> more surely than the light of noon
> to where He waited for me.[8]

---

8 St John of the Cross, *The Dark Night*, from *The Collected Works of St John of the Cross* translated by Kieran Kavanagh ocd and Otilio Rodriguez ocd, ICS Publications, Washington 1979, pp. 296-7.

4
This is my body

During my retreat in August 1984, contemplating Jesus in his agony in the garden (Luke 22:39–44), I was overwhelmed by a new realisation:

> *As I contemplated you on the ground, my heart cried out 'My God!' – a prayer that comes spontaneously when a situation is utterly beyond me. Then I saw that you are my God – my God lying in agony in the dust of the earth. There is no other God to whom I can appeal – only you, my agonising crucified God. And I just wanted to hold you, to be with you in your emptying of yourself, knowing I could only be there, empty of anything that could ease your pain, but with love, love that is able to go beyond the repulsive agony and see only you. I prayed that I might be poured out with you, for you, in loving adoration. O my God! O my God!* 24.8.1984

Jesus is drawing me into his passion through his hours of darkness in Gethsemane and on the Cross. But then came the realisation that the reverse is just as true:

> *At Mass tonight, Brian spoke of how nothing in our human experience is foreign to you. And I remembered the young girl, feeling trapped in the hole of poverty, crying in anguish in the night. O my God – You were there, with her, in her, You, the All-Holy God-become-man. That was also your agony, and that is why, when I took that experience to you recently and asked you to speak to me in it, you took me to the garden. And it was You crying out 'My God, my God, why have you forsaken me?' when I was plunged into the dark night of the non-existence of my God. O my God!* 24.8.1984

One by one, all the major dark and distressing experiences of my life came back to me, and, with them, the realisation that in each of them Jesus was with me, in me, experiencing them in me. And I thought I had been abandoned by him! The final few lines of this entry bring it all together:

> *There is nothing in my life that you do not live in me. Even my sin is not beyond your all-embracing goodness. If that is so, there is no need for fear when there seems nowhere to place my next step. Simply trust, trust absolutely – it is the Lord! Is adoration, then, the prayer of absolute trust in the One who emptied himself in loving adoration of the Father? O my God! This is utterly beyond my understanding! utterly beyond my capacity! And yet... You, in me, are giving me a glimpse of the depth of the mystery of your love.* 24.8.1984

The realisation of Christ's oneness with us in all our experiences came to me in a very different way some years earlier. The journal entry begins with I am my Beloved, a quote which initially puzzled me. My reflection on it takes me to what at first reading seems a surprising direction:

> *But then it dawned: this is the same as the awareness within me that I am sinful, suffering humanity. A deep pain and sorrow have lodged in my heart – I am the hostages in Teheran and the students who are holding them hostage. I am the baby aborted and the mother and doctor who have aborted it. I am the Vietnamese withholding food from the Kampucheans who are starving and I am the refugee. Somehow it is all present in me and I cry to the Lord for his healing, redeeming power for humanity. Lord have mercy on me, a sinner.* 5.12.1979

It is only now, as I reflect on these journal entries, that I see that these two experiences are two sides of the one reality. If I am the Beloved and the Beloved suffers in my suffering, the same Beloved suffers in all human suffering and, in the Beloved, I am one with suffering humanity. And together with the Beloved, I am to pour out in my life the infinite unconditional love and compassion that God pours out on me. The Beloved makes me like a clear crystal, totally open to the light and totally open to let that light flow through to whatever is around it.

Reading these journal entries all these years later, I am astounded at their profound depth. Awe silences me. Such grace, such amazing grace: This is Eucharist, my body given for you!

5
Drawn into crucified love

Graced with such amazing grace as I was, I was not lifted out of my wounded humanity. I continued to experience all the ups and downs, reactions, disappointments, jealousies, self-centredness, fears, doubts, poor self-worth, projections and so on, that were at the core of my struggles and pain. But by the mid-1980s, these did not drag me into the depths as they had in previous years. I was learning to question my reactions, to look for their deeper source, which usually had very little to do with the incident that gave rise to it.

I could appreciate what St Paul wrote to the Corinthians. After experiencing great revelations and visions, he was given a 'thorn in the flesh' which the Lord did not remove from him, despite his pleading. Rather he learnt that 'My grace is sufficient for you, for power is made perfect in weakness' (2 Corinthians 12:8).

As I moved through my midlife years and grew in self-knowledge, I was able to look more deeply into the root of the sense of alienation, of not quite belonging. When I allowed myself to connect with what was going on within me, I found I was again the lonely migrant child, isolated, alien, disappointed, hurting and with broken dreams. She was unable to express her experiences, so buried them deep down inside herself. In order to belong, she tried to be what she thought people expected her to be.

While I was no longer this child, my deep-down feeling of not being good enough was a carry-over from the child I was. It alienated me, but my alienation was not because I was a migrant who could not find herself at home in her adopted country. I was alienated from the home within, from myself. Until I found my home within myself, I could not be really at home anywhere; until I made my peace with the Corrie God made me to be, accepting her and embracing her with the same unconditional love with which God accepts and embraces me, I remained an alien.

All my efforts to conform to what I thought I was expected to be resulted in my living a lie.[9] 'The truth will make you free.' The truth that sets me free is the truth of myself,[10] my identity in Christ. I didn't know this at the time. The entrance to my true self was locked, and could only be unlocked, in the experience of my brokenness, weakness and sinfulness. In earlier years, I thought I had to become a saint before I could enter into union with God. But no! It is in and through my weak and broken self, in the dark night of Crucified Love – his, and also mine – that I am drawn into union with the Beloved. It is all God's work,[11] the work of grace, graciously poured out in us in the Holy Spirit who has been given to us (cf. Romans 5:5).

Gradually, I began to experience a renewed strength, something of a rebirth after a long dark night. During that dark night, growth, healing and a process of transformation was taking place, unseen while it was happening, but evident in how I now experienced myself. I felt like a butterfly emerging from its cocoon. I was still fragile, and, like Jeremiah when God called him to his prophetic mission, I felt still a child. But I took courage from God's saying to him, 'Don't say I am a child... I am putting my words into your mouth' (Jeremiah 1:6-7). Whatever the mission entrusted to me, God would give me whatever I need to carry it out. During my retreat in July-August that year (1986), a verse from Hosea arrested my attention:

I will lure her into the wilderness and speak to her heart (Hosea 2:14).

This luring can be scary. It can take me to a point of no return. Yet, even while I resist, I desire to be lured, to be seduced by the

---

9 See Sebastian Moore, *The Crucified is no Stranger*, Darton, Longman & Todd, London 1977. In this book Moore explores with powerful insight the mystery of sin rooted in our refusal to accept our true identity as a form of self-crucifixion which is revealed and forgiven in the Crucified Christ.
10 See James Finley, *Merton's Palace of Nowhere, A Search for God Through Awareness of the True Self*, Ave Maria Press, Notre Dame, Indiana, 1978. This book spoke powerfully to me at this stage of my life.
11 2 Corinthians 5:18-19. In his letters, Paul writes again and again of the astounding graciousness of God who uses our sinfulness to enter our lives and in mercy transform them into grace. This was his experience on the road to Damascus.

Lord. I pray, 'Lead thou me on, Lord, my Beloved'. My Beloved? I wondered whether I really did love God. Again, my familiarity with the scriptures brings a response:

> *How could I give you up, Corrie? My whole being recoils from it. I have loved you with an everlasting love, from the beginning, now and forever. O God, my God, my Jesus, my Beloved. What can I say? I long to love you, to be wholly yours forever.* 30.7.1986

This love is not confined to God-and-me. I share God's love with billions of people, each of whom is known and loved as personally as I believe God loves me. Countless among these people are in darkness, pain, even despair:

> *If I am really drawn into your love, I must also be drawn to them. It is as though my love for you is not just mine, but the human families of which I am a member. You ache for this human family, and in it you are crucified yet again. Thinking of all the people who suffer and are oppressed in one way or another, I said:*
> *– Lord, what can I do?*
> *– Nothing!*
> *– Nothing? Then I might as well go running barefoot in the grass!*
> *– No indeed! You must stay here, with the suffering people. Be as powerless as I am. And love them. This is the only hope they have.*
> *It strikes me that I always want to do something, even if only to put on a band-aid to cover the sore. You are saying that real love is to bleed with them. I hardly dare to write it. Is that what it means to be crucified with you?*
> *This means I must surrender my private little world, the world to which I can retire and from which I can shut out what I want to shut out. Taking down the gates to that world feels like a great burden: I have to do something about their pain. But no. Your invitation is to be with them, powerless as you are powerless in their powerlessness,*

and there to love them as you love me and as you love them. Dear Lord, to take up that kind of mission is beyond me. If this is what you are really asking, grant me also the 'Yes' to living it out day by day.   31.7.1986

I have always been a doer. I tended to value myself by the work I did, by how useful I was to others. Now the Lord was telling me that the heart of the Gospel mission is the willingness to be powerless with the powerless, to suffer with the suffering, to be with them in love, the same love with which God, in Jesus, loves us, even to death on the cross.

With that awareness, I sat with the crucifix and prayed:

Open me, my Love, to the depths of your crucified love.

Those depths included the sense of God's abandoning me: 'My God, my God, why have you forsaken me?' Then the dawning realisation:

'I can't help you either when you are on the cross. My body is nailed there. You will have to simply stay there. Yet you will know that I am crucified beside you, travelling my own desolate road as you travel yours. That will have to be enough for you.'

Later I wrote:

If you were not crucified, it would not be so hard to dismantle the gates to my private world. I don't need protection from a love that doesn't know crucifixion. But you invite me into the depths of your crucified love; you invite me to open myself up so that you can enter my inner sanctuary as Crucified Love. When I say yes to that, I no longer have a sanctuary – a refuge. I can no longer escape. Yet it will be truly a sanctuary, a sacred place where you live and in which you will make me one with yourself, yourself as crucified love.   1.8.1986

I came to realise that I needed Christ to be Crucified Love, for Crucified Love to abide in my inner sanctuary, and for my sanctuary to be open to people in pain so that there they may meet Christ, the crucified powerless One who is Love. I longed for the Lord to embed me in the mystery of which I caught a glimpse in that retreat, so that I might never forget it or lose sight of it.

Reading the above may evoke an image of Jesus and me in face-to-face conversations. The experience was far from that. I don't know that I experienced anything, at least in any perceivable way. My prayer and meditation seemed silent, empty, like non-events. It is only as I take up my pen to write, listening within for what may come, that these things emerge, and I am astounded by them. Taking up journal writing has been one of the most powerful gifts of my life, and the impulse of it came out of 'nowhere', an impulse from the Spirit in a time of confusion.

The later months of 1986 were filled with work, while my inner life continue to be filled with emptiness and tears. I continued to pray that I be drawn more deeply into Christ's crucified love. One day it occurred to me:

> *I also need to be drawn into the depth of my own crucified love – of which I am the crucifier. There I will find myself also in your love.*   4.11.1986

This was a moment of yet further realisation that, in rejecting myself, I was crucifying myself, and crucifying the Christ in me!

◇◇◇

At some stage during these years, an active imagination exercise took me to a cave which I needed to enter. At the entrance to the cave were two fierce-looking monsters which would not let me pass. The one on the left turned out to be my ambitious controlling ego self. When I faced it eye to eye, I saw the emptiness of its power. While scary, I saw it could not master me. The monster on the right was a combination of my fears, with its arsenal of guilt, shame and self-doubt, things about myself I tried to hide even from myself. This one would not let me pass. It held me in its grip. As I stood there, wondering how I could pass it, a little child appeared, took me by the hand and led me into the cave, ignoring the monsters. There I found Jesus waiting for me, together with my true identity, my real self.

The two monsters frequently come to mind as I write this part of my story. Facing these monsters is at the core of every human drama. During the years covered by this part of my story, I came to recognise these monsters, and learned how to deal with them. Even though I know they are my own creation, they continue to be a shadowy presence, hell-bound to prevent my entering that sacred cave. But the child in me will lead me where my heart longs to be: 'Unless you become like a little child, you cannot enter the kingdom of heaven' (Matthew 18:2).

Part IV

The Red Centre

1
Transitions

On 26 January 1987, I left Melbourne for South Australia.

The four of us who would be the Whyalla community that year drove to Adelaide. As the conversation gave way to silent companionship, I reflected on that mysterious something that is my relationship with God. Who is God, the Other in that relationship? That night in Adelaide I wrote in my journal:

I find myself aware of the God I don't believe in:

What I used to believe about God,
I no longer believe.
I do not believe in a God who solves my problems,
shields me from pain and heals me,
because I believe God has given me the capacity
to deal with my problems, walk in my pain
and come to healing.
I do not believe in a God who changes people,
because God has planted deep within each of us
the capacity to work for our own change.
I do not even believe in a God who is compassionate,
merciful and forgiving,
because what I and others need
is to connect with our own compassion,
mercy and forgiveness.

Yet deep within me there is God
who isn't these things,
but energises them in me.
God seems to be saying I don't need him –
and I don't.
And yet God knows I do need him
to be all these for me and in me.
But for my own life-growth
God mustn't be/do them.

> *And so I end up to being able to say*
> *almost nothing about God,*
> *and believing I'm not sure what –*
> *only with some idea of what God is not.*   26.1.1987

That is a profound change in my relationship with God, from what it was in earlier years. I used to throw all my needs, pain and worries onto God, like a child wanting mummy to kiss her better. But that mummy God is gone. Many years earlier I heard the Lord say:

> *Will you go to the ends of the earth with me without me?*

At the time I responded, *Yes*, not quite knowing what I was being asked. Now I know that from here on, I am thrown onto my own resources, God-given, yes, and able to seek support and wisdom from others, yes. But it is up to me to draw on those resources in whatever life should serve up to me. I have to be my own person, standing on my own feet.

This new way of being also impacts on my relationship with the Church. I need to let go of my expectations that the Church be the community so beautifully described in the scriptures and its ecclesiology. My eyes were being opened to the power structures of the hierarchical institution, disempowering laity and particularly women and their contribution to its life. Like the prophets of old, I began to experience myself as standing outside it, even while remaining within the fold.

In the four years I spent in Whyalla and the Port Pirie Diocese, my confidence in the new life that had been growing in me gradually deepened. The mission imperative that energised my earlier years was re-ignited in a new and deeper way. Mission is who I am and what I have become through the power of the Gospel.

2
Becoming embedded in country

The six-hour drive from Adelaide to Whyalla gives me my first look at the country in which I will live and work for the next four years. It seems to me the most desolate, God-forsaken country I have ever seen.

Over the following weeks and months, as I travelled the length and breadth of that vast Diocese, the country claimed me as its own. It worked its way into my heart and into the marrow of my bones, evoking a sense of wonder and awe, and yes, of kinship: the green of the vineyards and orchards of the Riverland, the rugged Flinders Ranges with their colourful formations and lush gorges, snaking their way some 400 kilometres through that otherwise dry and almost level land, the sheep and wheat country of the Eyre Peninsula, the red soils and grey saltbush of the inland, the coastal regions and fishing towns.

The country took me deeper into the mystery of creation, life, growth, and the Mystery we call God. It also taught me something about the desert experience. In 1989, Judith Thomson rsj and I did a trip to Coober Pedy. This was her first visit to the inland. While there, she led a retreat day for a group of women. Speaking to their experience of God's seeming absence, she compared it to the desert surrounds of Coober Pedy. Noticing that this didn't register with the women, she asked, 'Don't you experience this country as desert?' No, they did not. 'When you first came here, did it seem like a desert then?' Yes! As they thought back, they recognised that had been their experience. In that moment, I realised that a desert is only a desert as long as we don't find life there. Once we find life there, everything changes. This is also my inner experience. This is why God's absence no longer caused me anxiety. I know the desert journey holds life for me, even though I can't see it at the time. I recognise it in retrospect, when I become aware of the growth that has happened in me as life took me through the desert experience.

I asked myself, 'What nourishes life in me?' My response came immediately:

The whole of creation nourishes me. It is sacrament to me. The experience of the vastness of this land gives me a sense that I am on the verge of something momentous. This land gives me a different sense of space in which there arises in me a call, or maybe a promise, not yet clear, but awakening a sense of anticipation, waiting for I know not what...

Once in a while, sometimes in a long, long while, a miracle happens: the desert is blessed with copious rain. Almost immediately, the country stirs into life and is transformed into a carpet of colour – greys and greens, whites and golds, pink and purples, reds and blues – a riotous display of wild-flowers. It lasts only a few short weeks, just long enough for seed to form and mature. The seed falls to the ground and lies dormant in the hot dry red sandy soil until the next miracle of rain. Similarly in my inner desert experiences: brief moments of profound knowing, lifting me into a new sense of the Divine Mystery and who I am in that Mystery. Then I find myself back in the desert. But the seeds of such brief experiences live on, working their transformation in the roots of my being.

The natural environment touches me at all levels of myself. One time, while driving over the mountain range from Ringarooma to Fingal in Tasmania, I rounded a bend and was faced with the denuded flank of a clear-felled mountainside, its soils exposed to erosion by the elements. A pain shot through me, as though the skin of my chest was scoured off, leaving it raw and bleeding. What, oh, what are we doing, that we treat our Earth so appallingly! Where is our reverence for its sustaining ecology?

About this time, I wrote a poem:

*Walk softly on the Earth
she is your mother
nurturing
bringing to birth
we have no other.
Creator's heart
the Earth's and ours
all beat as one*

and unite
their vital powers
a blessed trinity.

But –
rape the womb
that gave you birth
devour the breast that feeds –
all Earth's life
breaks down and wastes –
to death your mother bleeds.   14.11.1988

The natural environment is the stuff of poetry and prayer, both modern and ancient. The psalmist sings, 'Let the rivers clap their hands, the mountains shout with them for joy, for the Lord for he comes' (Psalm 98). Jesus grew up with prayers like this. He was intimately familiar with the Earth which birthed the prayer-poems of psalmists. In his teachings, he drew on images from nature and from the lives of his listeners. They understood what he was talking about… except – he always gave his parables that unexpected twist, challenging them to look again at their assumptions, to see what they had not seen before.

If this land means so much to me, how much more does it mean to Australia's First Peoples. For them, Country is mother, it has given them birth and constantly sustains them. It is their identity, their culture, their spirituality. It is the home of their ancestors, embedded with their ancient wisdom stories.

The way our First Peoples lived and expressed their cultures was very different from the colonisers' knowledge and imagination. The latter dismissed even the possibility that Indigenous Peoples and their way of life might have something of value to offer the newcomers. To them, the Aboriginal people were savages who hunted and gathered to survive, who had no use for the land. There was no acknowledgment that they owned the land.[12] The newcomers presumed they had a right to it. We have a long way to go to right the wrongs of our history.

---

12 Aboriginal people don't own the land, country owns *them*. It is where they belong.

3
Back to my roots

An Aboriginal Elder once said to me, 'You will never know who you are until you go back to your own country'. This is certainly the experience of our Aboriginal people. Their relationship to Country encompasses everything from which they draw their identity, their sense of meaning and belonging, their spirit, spirituality, their ancestors and the wisdom of their traditions. The depth of that relationship with Country is beyond my understanding, though I deeply respect it.

And what about me? Do I need to go back to my own country in order to know who I am? I am aware of how Australia has claimed me for itself. Every part of the country in which I have lived or visited has nourished me with its rugged beauty, from the mountains of Tasmania to the Great Outback. Australia is deeply embedded in me, and I am embedded in the country. It draws me into its ancient mystery, enriches my sense of the sacred and nourishes my spirit. The country has 'grown' me. I feel at home in Australia, and at home within myself in Australia. I am amazingly gifted by my adopted country.

It came as a surprise then, when in 1991, I began to feel a yen to visit the land of my birth. It was forty years since my family had left Holland to start a new life in Australia. And now, this yen arises! What prompted it? As I pondered this, I realised that it came from the desire to understand my roots, to know my Dutch heritage. Had I lost touch with it altogether or was it still part of me?

I wrote to our leadership team about my desire to visit the Netherlands. They encouraged me to go, suggesting I take three months. Three months! It seemed a long time to spend there, but maybe I would need that length of time if I was to really experience my Dutch heritage from my deeper sense of self.

I flew with Air Olympic to Athens, surrounded by Greek conversation. On my connecting flight to Amsterdam, I was surrounded by Dutch people, returning home after holidaying in Greece. This gave me opportunity to attune myself to the language which I had hardly spoken in over thirty years.

When the plane broke through the clouds above Holland, I was amazed to see acres and acres of cultivated land and glass houses. With a population of around sixteen million in a country about two-thirds the size of Tasmania, I didn't expect to be greeted with a rural landscape.

Once off the plane, I collected my luggage and walked through customs. A cursory check of my passport, and I was through the door into the reception area. I heard 'Daar is ze'(There she is). My aunt Rita and cousins Gonnie and Annie were there to welcome me with hugs and kisses all round. We found a place to sit down with a cool drink and chat for about half an hour. I was amazed at how easily I slipped back into Dutch, though my vocabulary was rather limited.

Over the next eighty days, I immersed myself in the life of the country. Times spent with various members of my very large extended family gave me a great range of experiences. Everywhere I went, I was welcomed with warm and generous hospitality. Uncles, aunts and cousins invited me to stay with them in their homes and took me into their workplaces. I visited museums and art galleries, read history and immersed myself in the life and culture of my people, hungry to discover just what it was to be Dutch.

I had been in the Netherlands about seven weeks when, while staying with Toon and Wil van den Bosch and their family, Toon asked me had I been to the Delta Works. Delta Works? What are they? I had not heard of the Delta Works. Toon and Wil offered to take me there and I learnt the remarkable story of those works.

In January 1953, there was a disastrous flood that inundated the province of Zeeland and the southern islands of the province of South Holland. A king tide, backed by gale-force winds coming from the west, coincided with the rivers, in full spate from melting snows, flowing from the east. Over 1,800 people lost their lives, together with a huge loss of live-stock and property. It was a national disaster. Throughout the country, people offered hospitality to those who had lost everything, and to stock that escaped the waters. The government set up a commission to look into the factors that brought about the disaster and to come up with a plan to prevent such catastrophes in the future. The result was the creation of the Delta Works.

My visit to the Delta Works clinched something for me, bringing into focus what I sought to know and understand. My journal tells of this experience:

> *The commission came up with a bold plan – to build dams, bridges and sluice gates that would prevent the waters of the sea from overwhelming the waters and islands of Zeeland and Zuid Holland. It took thirty years to complete this gigantic project. The greatest challenge was to create a storm surge barrier in the (river) Oosterschelde. The object was to allow sea water free flow into the Oost Schelde, conserving the habitat of flora, fauna and sea life, and also to have the capacity to hold back the sea in abnormally high tides and storm floods. Thus Neeltje Jan was conceived, a project of such proportions and daring, the technology to carry it out had yet to be invented.*
>
> *As we watched a film showing, step by step, the design and realisation of the project, I found myself deeply moved in a way I can't explain. Then we went to see the storm barriers themselves. An expo showed the total project, the development of the dams and gates along the seaboard, the sluice gates up the rivers. A section showed the first known struggles to shut out the sea with dikes in Roman times, and a film of the 1953 floods. Again, I was deeply moved and fought back the tears and sobs that welled up in me.*
>
> *What is it that so deeply touches and moves me? Yes, there was the suffering on the faces of the victims of that disaster, the loss of loved ones and everything they had. All these were heartrending. But there was something else: the courage and determination to fight back, to take on the power of the elements, of sea and storm winds, and wrest back their land, rebuild their homes, farms and towns, metres below sea level. Here I touched – or rather, was touched by – that 'something' in the national character that is uniquely, personally Dutch. My parents showed*

> *something of it in the face of adversities they experienced in our early years in Australia. Something of that same metal is in me. It is a strength, but also...*
>
> *The message of both films, and of the works themselves, is that the disaster of 1953 will never happen again. I shuddered as I heard that stated at the conclusion of each film. I pray that this may be so, but 'never' is an enormous claim which, maybe, overlooks the limits of our potential. Please God, never again! And I do not even know how I understand that prayer.*

From the Delta Works we headed inland, to Oirschot in Brabant, where I had arranged to make my annual retreat. The timing could not have been better. I needed space and quiet to ponder and assimilate what had touched me so deeply at the Delta Works. In that experience I touched something at the core of the Dutch character: the sheer dogged determination with which my people have struggled with the waters that constantly threatened to invade the land. Again and again throughout history their lands were flooded. Countless people lost their lives as flood waters inundated the land yet again! Yet, as often as floods destroyed their homes and livelihoods, so often they set about rebuilding and reinforcing the dikes, building sluice gates and locks to slow down the flow of rivers and hold back the tides, pumping the waters from their polders so they could rebuild their homes and farms. There is, in the Dutch character, a refusal to give in, an unyielding determination to find ways to protect their land and people from the ever-threatening waters.

That determination also comes through in the direct way the Dutch speak. When I listened to Dutch conversations with my Australian ears, people sometimes sounded arrogant or dogmatic. But listening with my Dutch ears, that is just the way they speak, particularly when they feel passionately about the subject matter under discussion. People are not necessarily offended when another contradicts their strongly stated views, though they will argue their case. They know that whatever they know won't be the final word on a topic. The Delta Works are the final word for now, hence the audacious statements that the disaster of 1953 can never happen again.

After I returned Australia, I wrote some reflections on the experience:

> *What did I discover of the Dutch character and way of life? There are many beautiful dimensions to it: their strong family bonds, their 'gezelligheid',[13] their industriousness, their hospitality and generosity, their social and environmental consciousness, their dogged determination, and so on. Together with this, I noticed their preoccupation with money, material security and the cost of things. There is a certain frugality in their approach to things. They are not afraid of spending money, but are careful about how they spend it. I guess that is why the people are materially so well off. They do not readily take unsecure risks, letting go of one position before they can put a foot firmly on another.*
>
> *I wonder whether their security in the material holds them back from discovering and developing other dimensions of life. My innate tendency is also such. But I have been blessed in having been in situations about which I had no guarantee of security. I have had opportunity to branch out into many new challenges and have grown and developed through these experiences.*   19.10.1992

In the light of my visit to the Netherlands, what has my Australian experience given me? Without trying to detail this, I think my experience here has enlarged my world greatly. It also has given me a spirit of freedom to embrace new experiences, to try new things, to move to new places, geographically and psychologically. One of my cousins is a doctor, a GP. He told me he sometimes feels he would like to do something different. When I asked him what stopped him, he looked at me in amazement. Changing one's profession was unheard of in his world.

---

[13] There is no English expression that quite translates this Dutch word. It is an atmosphere of homeliness, companionship, warmth, comfort, cozy, inviting...

While appreciating the strengths of my Dutch heritage, I also experienced their shadow side. Tendencies such as my determination, persistence, work ethic, can become driving energies that enslave me. Frugality can become meanness. Directness of speech can be offensive to others. Over the years, I have become more aware of how these tendencies come to the fore, especially in the heat of the moment, or when the pressure is on.

To return to the question with which I began this chapter, was the Aboriginal Elder right when he told me I would need to go back to my own country in order to know my true identity? During my time in the Netherlands and reflecting on my experience there since my return, I certainly came to some understanding of my Dutch heritage, and to recognise its formative influence on me. Beyond that, I also have an Australian identity and a sense of belonging in this country. This land has also had an enormous formative influence on me. It seems to me that my sense of identity has continued to emerge in relation to Country wherever I am. But my identity is not tied to or limited by any one place. Having lived in many places in five Australian States, I find myself at home wherever I am. Today there is a cosmic dimension to my at-homeness. We belong to, and are part of, the Universe. Our history goes back to some fourteen billion years. How mind-blowing it that!

4
Women's business

During my years in the Port Pirie Diocese, I grew to appreciate the qualities I bring to our mission *as a woman*. Feminine images became very significant in my relationship with Jesus and in shaping my understanding of how I am to be with people. This came powerfully to me during a retreat:

> *I went to John's Gospel to hear your invitation: 'If anyone thirsts, let her come to me. Let the person come and drink who believes in me. As the scripture says, from his breast shall flow fountains of living water' (John 7:37-38). What a beautiful feminine image – the tender intimacy between mother and child. I stayed in contemplation ...*

Later that same day:

> *I was doing some knitting and the image of your breasts, flowing with living water came back to me, together with the invitation, 'Come and drink'. I felt repulsed. While the image of a mother breast-feeding her child is so moving for me, when you invited me to be that child, I could not come and drink.*   20.1.1988

For the next couple of days, I remained in that impasse: what was it that prevented me from drinking at Jesus' breast? Whatever I took as the focus for meditation, I continually found myself back at my inability to respond to Jesus' invitation to drink. Then:

> *I went to the well at Sychar – Jacob's well: 'If you only knew what God is offering, and who it is that is asking you for a drink, you would have been the one to ask, and he would have given you living water' (John 4:10). His voice stirs up deep longings. The conversation with the woman went on, but it left me behind. When she left, I was alone with Jesus and sat down beside him. He took my hand.*

> *'Do <u>you</u> know the gift of God?'*
> *'I do and I don't... I think I fail to recognise it for what it really is.'*
> *'If you want to receive the gift of God, you need to receive all of yourself.'*
> *As he said this, I remembered my history, aspects of myself which made for difficulty in relating, times when I down-played aspects of my giftedness because they may not be understood or accepted. I sat silently in that awareness. Suddenly he said, 'Come and drink', and offered me his breast. I lay my head in his arm and drank. I was inundated with love and peace.* 22.4.1988

It isn't enough to drink that living water. He sent me to nurture people from my breast, the people I live with and work among. I notice a recurring pattern here: whatever I experience in my relationship with Jesus is meant to shape the way I am to be with people. In this case, what might it mean to nurture people from my breast? I would have to wait and see.

A few weeks later:

> *I was reminded of your commission to go out, nurturing people from my breast. This is what I do when I share what has truly become my own, what has become my flesh and my blood, to be turned into milk to nurture others. That means I need to trust what has been given: the truth of myself, the truth in myself, and stand firmly on that, for that is the fruit of the Spirit in me.* 15.6.1987

Later that year:

> *To become compassion! Compassion is who you are, the name you revealed to Moses. Compassion is who you enable me to become. Compassion seems to come from the womb,[14] the place where new life is conceived and*

---
14 I had read somewhere that the Hebrew word for compassion, Rachamim, has 'womb' in its root.

nurtured, where motherhood is born. Compassion is the milk in my breast from which I am to feed your lambs and sheep.

Compassion was certainly called for: I was frequently in touch with people in their sufferings – with the family whose son committed suicide, with the young girl unable to find a job, with farmers facing bankruptcy because of exorbitant interest rates on their loans, with the woman suffering flashbacks of horrific abuse she had suffered as a child, with the Vietnam veteran suffering the effects of exposure to agent orange, with Wayne asking for a meal and apologising again and again for having to ask...

> *I spent the whole day visiting: every person with a story of struggle or grief. Have I been Good News to them? There is so much need for a compassionate listener, for someone who can share their burdens, even if only for a little while. Hopefully, just that will give them new heart, new hope.*
> 31.7.1990

People such as those mentioned here made me more and more aware of the systems of injustice we human beings create. Once created, these systems enslave us, though we can remain largely unconscious of that fact. It is the poor and disadvantaged who suffer most.

During these years I also became aware of the relationship between what we now call eco justice and social justice. The impoverishment of the Earth and the impoverishment of people go hand in hand. Both are the result of greed for wealth and power. I ponder, is there another way?

> *How can we presume to own land or water? I have often thought that our practice of buying and selling Earth, or part of it, is at the root of much evil in our world. We speak of Australia as our Commonwealth, but it is in the hands of the few. There are millions of refugees on Earth, and we deny them a place to live. They are confined to refugee camps, or forcefully repatriated to face what they sought*

> to escape. *The Earth, our country, is God's creation, to be shared by all creation for the life of the world.*
>
> *Is it possible for us to organise our society without private ownership of land, rivers and seas?*[15] *If all **were** commonwealth, land could be leased, but only to those who live on it and earn their living from it. No one could amass land. Anyone not taking proper care of the land would have his or her lease terminated, and so on. Could we devise a system that works in favour of every person? And could we persuade people to adopt such a system in a climate which tells them that more is better, that ownership decides the value of a person, that wealth is power? 'Blessed are the poor in spirit' (Matthew 5:3).*   30.7.1990

Since time immemorial, women have been seen as deeply connected to the Earth. Both bring forth and nurture life. The Earth is seen as feminine, as mother. Patriarchal cultures often assume that they have a right to dominate and exercise power over women and nature, with the result that women and nature are often used and abused.[16] There is a close relationship between advocating for more sustainable ways of caring for the Earth and its eco-systems, and working for the recognition of women's dignity and liberation.

Working on the diocesan Renew[17] team, I met the patriarchal culture close-up. The other half of the team was a priest but I never felt we were on an equal footing. While he saw himself as appreciating women's role in the Church, he was not aware how the patriarchal

---

15 Indigenous cultures have never included private ownership of land. They lived and worked communally on their territories.

16 I want to stress here that patriarchy refers to a culture, not specifically to men. Both men and women can be patriarchal in their thinking and their ways of relating. Conversely, both men and women can approach women and nature with reverence and respect.

17 Renew was a three-year parish-based renewal program, consisting of six 'seasons', two a year, each of four weeks duration. The program included small groups of people meeting weekly, reflecting on the Gospel reading for the following Sunday, relating it to their daily lives. Priests and liturgy groups were encouraged to develop the theme of each week in the Sunday liturgies and parish schools were encouraged to include the themes in their religious education curriculum. Towards the end of each year, a diocesan festival brought people together from the whole Diocese.

culture influenced his way of relating with me. I often felt he didn't understand and trust what I brought to the work.

When I returned from summer holidays in late January 1989, I learned that, at his instigation, while remaining the director of Renew, he was appointed parish priest of a town that was a five-hour drive from Whyalla. I was shocked that this decision had been taken without any discussion with me or on how it would impact on my role in the work of Renew. A few days later, at our first team meeting for the year, he told me that the office we had been using was needed by the parish. Again, there had been no discussion with me. I was presented with the fait accompli. It was taken for granted that I would adapt. That's what was – and often still is – expected of women in the Church. I didn't challenge the new arrangements. In the moment, it didn't occur to me that I *could* challenge or object. I accepted them, though not without being dismayed about it.

While I was conscious of the impact a patriarchal culture had on women, psychologically I was also part of that culture. In not speaking up in situations such as the above, we women are complicit in maintaining that culture. If the culture is to change, we need to enter the struggle and address the assumptions and thinking that underpin it. Men don't experience patriarchy like women do. Not until women take their place alongside men on an equal footing, will men realise that they too are impoverished in an all-male hierarchical structure in the Church and society.

As I write this, it occurs to me how often popes and bishops speak of 'Holy Mother Church'. Yet their insistence on right beliefs, law and morality is a travesty of mothering. It excludes those it considers sinners, those who do not, or cannot, live up to their demands. This emphasis by the Church's leadership has created a class system in which authority is vested in an all-male ordained hierarchy, increasingly centralised in Rome, to the neglect of the inclusiveness of Jesus' 'mothering', especially of the people on the periphery, the social outcasts and people the authorities of his days considered sinners. A true mother does not cast out the child with special needs or those who misbehave. It took a Pope Francis to bring Jesus' way of mothering back to the centre where it belongs, though today's equivalent of the scribes and pharisees in the Church vehemently disagree with him. The feminine is at the heart of Jesus' mission, together with a healthy masculine.

One area that has bugged me over the years is the almost exclusive masculine language of the Church's prayer and liturgy:

> *Jesus told us to call God 'Father'. This is surely a beautiful relational image. Yet in our time it is virtually the only name for God we use in prayer. Yes, there is 'Lord' too. Such titles convey something about our relationship with God. But neither is anywhere near adequate to indicate the mystery of God which is utterly beyond understanding and imagining. Sometimes I consciously use the pronoun 'she' of God. When I pray 'Our Mother', the feeling is entirely different from that of praying 'Our Father'. The father image conveys to me a God who stands outside of, over, or above creation. The mother image conveys a God who both surrounds all creation, as a womb surrounds the child she carries, and who permeates with her presence, creation in its deepest core.*
>
> *Our Church's liturgy is dominated by images of the God of power and might. It supports and legitimates the use of power in the Church and society. I think it is more true to the divine Mystery if we drop the power notion, and instead use the word love. For we do not experience God lording power over us. Rather we experience people lording God's power over us. The Prophet says, 'I have led you with the leading strings of love'. Love does not dominate. Love sets us free, that we might live and grow and become all we are and all we can be, together. Love empowers from within. From the deepest core of our being, we are permeated by God who is Love.* 9.2.1992

I played with the notion of God as mother, and wrote the following paraphrase of the Our Father:

> *Our Mother, who are deep within us and all around us,*
> *May your name be held sacred in our hearts and in all creation.*

May your empowering love be the energy enlivening all that is,
bringing the Universe and its inhabitants into your unity and harmony.
Help us this day to provide each other with our daily bread.
Forgive us our wrongs as we forgive those who wrong us.
Do not allow us to be tested beyond our capacity
but free us from the powers of evil.

This prayer gives me a very different feel of who God is, and of who I am in relation to God. Essential to that relationship is my relationship with every other person and with creation itself. I cannot be, nor be the person I am called to be, except in that three-fold relationship.

◇◇◇

Participating in a course on Art as Prayer, I experienced anew how negative feelings are transformed when I allow myself to be with them:

I didn't feel like going to the session tonight. I felt I had hit the pits, and it isn't the kind of space from which I want to face a group for sharing. But I went, knowing it is a good place from which to work with what's going on for me.
Val (the facilitator) had a series of black and white pictures spread out on the floor like a path. She invited us to walk the path and find the picture that drew our attention. The one I picked up seemed to have selected me, rather than the other way around. The impression it gave me was of someone heavily burdened. I sat with it for a few minutes, then decided to work with clay. I kneaded the clay into a ball. It became a large heavy rock. I moulded hands and arms carrying the rock. As I worked on that burden, the image began to change: a woman's pregnant belly, held in her arms. I wondered, what needs to come to birth in me? Later, someone in the group showed me the coloured version of the image in the book from which it came. It is entitled 'Firebird'. The dream that gave birth to the

> *picture spoke of a birthing ground, of generativity and birth:*
>
> In each age, an attempt is made to bring this symbol (the firebird) of the awakening and the initiation of humanity to birth... You who seek to embody the sacredness of God's creation in everyday life are, collectively, a womb in which the embryo of a new civilization has taken root.[18]   31.3.1992

The authors of the book have extended the meaning of the dream beyond what I had seen. For them, the woman in the image is symbolic of humanity, pregnant with its future. I am part of that collective womb in which a new consciousness is developing. This journey is not just about me as an individual.

The sense of being pregnant arose frequently in me through those years, though I didn't know what was gestating in me:

> *I am struck, as I've been a number of times in recent months, maybe years, by the yearning, the expectancy, almost a sense of promise, of a breakthrough into a new dimension of consciousness of being. As I sit with that sense today, I perceive it as something akin to the prophets' vision of a new order, a new heaven and a new earth, in which justice will reign with love and compassion. In the scriptures the prophetic images come mainly from men. Today, it seems that the mainstream of the prophetic movement comes from women.*   1.4.1992

---

18 Marcia S. Lauck and Deborah Koff-Chapin, *At the Pool of Wonder, Dreams and Visions of an Awakening Humanity*, Bear & Co. 1989.

5
The bread of wisdom

In 1991, I returned to Melbourne to continue my study in theology. During my years in South Australia, I often wondered what my theology studies could contribute to the experience of the people I lived and worked among. It all seemed too remote and heady. Returning to my studies, I brought a definite focus: theology had to arise from and speak to our human experience. It wasn't enough to take what lecturers and writers told me. I had to work it through until it revealed the deeper meaning of our human experience. My learning needed to be integrated with my inner life. It had to contribute to my relationship with God and to my relationships with people and with creation. Only then could knowledge become wisdom.

My dreams play a role in this as well. They can reveal to me aspects of my inner self of which I am unaware. Their meaning is not evident at first sight, but when I work the dream symbols, their meaning gradually reveals itself:

> *In my dream I reacted furiously to a conservative, 'other worldly' priest who had gone to Holland to get things for the coming confirmation, while right here in the parish, he has all the resources needed to do whatever is necessary, and to do so with beauty and dignity. Maybe it reflects my tendency to look to other people, or established ways, for what I need in life, instead of trusting the creative resources within and around me.*
>
> *As I reflect on this, I am reminded of an earlier dream of an ancient Bread that had been recovered at much cost, and which would leave the country if the university didn't take it. There is ancient wisdom in me – much more ancient than the external sources of wisdom I have encountered. If I don't accept the ancient, yet always fresh, Bread of Wisdom, it will be lost to me – and to the world.*

The ancient Bread of Wisdom within me needs to be in continual dialogue with the tradition of the Church, and the realities of our world. I frequently experienced a growing tension between the direction the Bread of Wisdom was leading me and what the institutional Church insisted upon. Its 'orthodoxy' seemed so remote from our lives and the actual world in which we live:

> *I went to the parish celebration of penance last night and came home feeling flat and untouched. It was obvious that an effort had been made in its preparation, but the resulting liturgy was hardly liturgy. We were silent throughout. The action before us did not move me. There was no sense of community celebration. It was a collective of individuals, focused on our individual selves. The symbols and symbolic gestures had potential to become movers of mind and heart, but they seemed disconnected and remained impotent. Where was our community consciousness? Where was our social sin? Where and how does a social–cultural–economic climate bind us together in sinfulness and impotence? Where and how do we contribute to that?*
>
> *We have a need for social conversion. The sorts of things we need to bring into celebrations of penance – our consumerism and materialism, the climate that creates a drug culture, the crime and violence in society, the waste and destruction of our environment, and so on. While individually we may not be involved in the behaviours that show up these things for what they are, nevertheless, we are part of the culture that produces them. Very subtly, we are caught up in that culture, deceived by it and we contribute to it. Lord, have mercy.*   10.4.1992

Speaking up in response to such experiences is the role of the prophet. It requires contemplative discernment in which the example and teaching of Jesus are the touchstone by which my understanding of that ancient Bread of Wisdom is tested and refined. Then that Wisdom can find expression in my life and my mission.

I am realising that women's way of doing theology is practical; it focuses on what we do, how we live, how we relate to others and to creation. If this is so, where does mystical experience fit? Some people seem to see an opposition between mysticism and action, as I read in an article:

> (The author) *emphasises the doing of the Gospel – the love of one another, inclusiveness in our relationships, justice, etc. She does not see mysticism as part of Gospel living. I disagree. We cannot be intimately related to God without being related to all of creation in God. As we become more aware of our being completely in the Divine Mystery, we know we are one with the whole of creation and especially with our fellow human beings. Then loving oneself is loving the other, and loving the other is loving God and loving oneself. It is all one.* 4.4.1992

I know this from experience. My love for people, my passion for justice and for the environment have grown and deepened as I have grown in my relationship with God. Again and again, my journal comments on the suffering of people in current situations of the violence, oppression, poverty in its myriad forms and the damage we cause to the natural world. That suffering touches me. I struggle with the realisation that I am part of the systems that create these conditions in the world, which give me the quality of life I enjoy. It is difficult to know how to really live justly in this world.

As my study time drew near its end, I reflected:

> *I am almost at the end of my course, and I feel as though I am really just ready to begin. I am beginning to recognise and trust my own insights, questions, wisdom and to express these confidently instead of hesitantly, apologetically or defensively. And I am open to receiving the broadening of another's critique on my insights and questions.* 8.6.1992

I had come to appreciate that there is a knowing of the heart that goes beyond words and ideas that I have studied. Such heart-knowing comes in moments of encounter, sometimes in a comment someone makes, sometimes in a situation in which I find myself, sometimes when I feel vulnerable and defensive, sometimes in a word of encouragement, sometimes in prayer and contemplation. In such moments of recognition, I find myself saying, 'But of course. Why haven't I seen this before?' Until this moment, it remained on the periphery of my awareness. Now that it has moved to the centre of my awareness, Word and life meet in me and bring theology to life. It transforms the way I experience life, people, and the whole of creation.

Part V

To know and be known

1
The world of dreams

In 1995, I did a month-long retreat at the Portiuncula Centre,[19] Toowoomba, Queensland, with Pat Quinn mss, as my guide.

I asked for two graces from this retreat: to be drawn into deeper communion with God, and to grow more fully into my humanity and know it in communion with the whole of creation. As I reflect on these two graces twenty-five years later, I see that they come to the same thing.

The way into both those graces came through the world of symbols accompanied by journal writing. Under Pat's guidance, I engaged with symbols coming from my dreams and sandplay meditations. These took me to a new level of understanding and relating to myself as well as to God.

Early in my retreat, I had a dream in which I met a magnificent lion. While I could admire it from a distance, I was also scared of it. Pat invited me to become the lion. When I did, the lion described itself as a magnificent creature, king of creatures, wild and free. Suddenly, it started to cry. It admitted that it wasn't free. It was a circus lion, tamed and trained to perform according to its master's directions.

That lion was me. All my life I had tried to be what I thought others wanted me to be. I had buried the wild and free aspects of myself. The lion showed me yet again what has become a refrain over the years: *Corrie, you need to let go of what you think you ought to be and become the woman God created you to be.* Towards the end of that retreat, the lion returned in another dream. This time it was lying relaxed against my body. I could feel its heartbeat and I was not afraid. This dream didn't resolve once and for all my inclination to 'perform' for others, nor my need for approval, acceptance and belonging which are its motivating forces. But its wisdom has stayed with me. When my

---

19 The Portiuncula is the little church restored by St Francis. It is located within the basilica in Assisi, Italy. For Pat Quinn mss, the Portiuncula symbolises the inner sanctuary of our hearts, an apt symbol for a centre focused on personal and spiritual growth.

pleaser takes over, the lion's wisdom calls me back to the place of inner integrity and truth, leading me to trust the authority inherent in those qualities.

In another dream, I met a migrant woman from Scandinavia who spoke very little English. She was a skilled spinner and weaver and was spinning some superfine wool. When I explored this dream, Pat suggested I dance the Spinner:

> *Pat put on some music, and I spun to its rhythm. Longer and longer grew the yarn, stretching into one long, smooth spinning movement. The rhythm took over. The dancer became the Divine Spinner and Weaver. I experienced her infinite tenderness and care as she fingered the texture of the wool and felt her way into the potential of me. Gently, she drew the thread, longer and longer. Then warp and weft, she wove it into strong, beautiful fabric, each single fibre so fragile, but the whole strong. Then she took me and wrapped herself in me like a cloak. I am the garment clothing the Divine. She wears me with love and pride.*

I wrote a dialogue with the Spinner and Weaver, listening to what she had to teach me. She asked me to look more closely at the fibres she spun, the fibres of myself. As I did:

> *I recognise some of them. There is the thundercloud black of my anger, and the brown of my newly discovered defiance. I see the crimson threads of my bleeding heart for the suffering of people. The green of envy is there, and the gold of joy. The purple threads of pain are there too – lots of them. And there are soft, strong threads of love in all the colours of the spectrum. There is the misty fibre of loneliness and the translucence of wonder and awe. My self-righteousness and vindictiveness are also included. And there's the rich red of passion and the white of integrity. My stubborn determination is there too, the colour of steel, and my creativity catching the light and refracting it in a thousand shades and forms. The longer I look, the more I see.*

She responds:

Every fibre is necessary for the work of art which is you. Every fibre adds to the beauty of the whole. Remember how tenderly I held and felt those fibres? I felt their texture, their softness or hardness, their flexibility and their rigidity, their warmth and coolness.

I am astonished and reply:

A lot of those fibres are aspects of myself I find hard to acknowledge, let alone accept. And you are pleased to wrap yourself in all of that?

She says:

Corrie, of course I am pleased – more than pleased, I delight in wrapping myself in you – the whole of you. You fix on those so-called negatives in isolation. I see them coming from a struggling heart, out of the threats and hurts and fears of your life. I feel them with you as I touch each fibre. I never thought of creating you without the full spectrum of human feelings, reactions and experiences. Without these, your so-called positives would be weak and anaemic. Even their colours would be insipid. It is the contrasts that give colours their full hues and vibrancy.

31.5.1995

Reading this dialogue some twenty-five years later, I reconnect with its profound impact on me. I tend to judge myself harshly when the so-called negatives arise in reaction to what is touching me in the moment. The Divine Weaver has a much more compassionate understanding of my human propensities than I have of myself. She sees deeper and knows my heart. Another powerful encounter with my feminine came through a sandplay. I created a wilderness space in the sandbox and put in it the figure of a woman, sitting still on the ground. I spoke to her, asking who she was. Her response came as prose-poem which I entitled Wisdom Woman:

To know and be known

*I am your still centre,
the silence deep within you.
You want to climb the mountain
and walk along the river.
But I, in my stillness,
find the mountain and the river in myself.
They are part of me and I of them.
I draw life from their inner reality
and they nourish and enlarge my spirit
simply by my being still in their presence.
I am the solitude within you,
the one who withdraws you
from the busy commerce of the outer life,
that you may touch and come to know
what it offers to your inner life.
I am the still waters which,
motionless,
reflect all the life and movement of the Universe.
I am the wisdom within you.
The wisdom others offer you
will only become your wisdom
when you discover it reflected
in the well at the centre of your being.
I gather and treasure
all the experiences of your life.
In you I ponder them
until they draw you into their inner meaning –
their truth –
which becomes your wisdom.
Nothing,
no experience of life
is too minor, too insignificant
for it to find a place
among the things I treasure for you.
Come, spend time with me
in quiet solitude and rest.*

> *Then, in not doing you will accomplish much;*
> *in not knowing you will understand a great deal;*
> *in not seeing you will perceive*
> *the hidden reality of everything;*
> *in not speaking you will become*
> *the Word that holds all being;*
> *and being apart, you will know yourself part of all.*
> *My name is Woman,*
> *the Breath of God.* 9.6.1995

My heart resonates with the beauty and profundity of her words. It is language of mysticism and poetry.

Later in that retreat, I was to meet this Woman again, in the yen to be a hermit, a yen that had been with me for many years. Pat suggested I give that yen a voice:

> *When she spoke, I recognised her as the Wisdom Woman, the mystic who spoke to me earlier in the retreat. This time, she spoke of being with the mystery at the heart of things – the seed with its potential for life; water – simply marvelling at the extraordinary element it is. She is the one, I realise, who brings me those unexpected experiences of a different level of awareness. There was tremendous energy in her voice – not the energy of busyness, but the energy of finding herself grounded in Mystery – the Mystery of being who she is within the Mystery of all Being. She has a sense of connectedness, of kinship with the world, with the Universe. I delighted in her voice.*
> 19.6.1995

The call to a hermit life was strong. As I reflected on it, I recognised that I am to carry my hermitage deep within, treasuring the contemplative dimension of my life as mission, while actively engaging with people and the wider world.

Upon reaching my late 70s, life itself presented me with an external hermitage: my present home where I live alone. Yet I have not withdrawn from involvements with people and the wider world beyond my home. Hospitality of mind and heart continues to take me into people's lives, whether it is going out to them, or welcoming them into my home. They are part of my contemplative way of life, nurturing me as I nurture them.

At the end of that long retreat, I wrote a poem in which I expressed some of the key experiences of those days:

*In the centre of the castle of Corrie
there is a small shrine in the form of a lotus flower
and within can be found a small space.
We should find who dwells there
and we should want to know her.*[20]

*So I asked,
Who is she who dwells
in the small shrine in the form of a lotus flower
in the centre of the castle of Corrie?
Whom should I want to know?*

*And a guide took me by the hand
and led me through memories and dreams,
through breath and symbols
into that small shrine in the form of a lotus flower
in the centre of the castle of Corrie.*

*And opening the way into that small space,
I found it vast as the universe:
The heavens and the earth are there,
and the sun and the moon and the stars.
Fire and lightning and wind are there,
and all the pain and anguish, the fears and darkness
that ever touched my life.
And all my longing and hope are there.
All that now is and all that has been,
all that is not and all that is yet to be
is in the small space in the small shrine
in the form of a lotus flower
in the centre of the castle of Corrie
And the One who dwells there*

---

20 The imagery of this poem comes from the Chandogya Upanishad.

*is weaving a garment
out of all that now is and all that has been
and all that is not;
a garment in which she delights to clothe herself,
which she wears with pride.
With the help of my companion and guide
I have met her who dwells
in the small space in the small shrine
in the form of a lotus flower
in the centre of the castle of Corrie.
Her name is Woman, the Breath of God.
And the whole Universe is in her
and she dwells within my heart.*   24.6.1995

At some stage during this long retreat, Pat asked me had I ever considered doing the counselling training course she and her team offered. The course would enable me to continue the deep inner work of these days. I replied that I didn't think that counselling was my gift. She chuckled: 'What do you think you have been doing in your sessions with me? You have taken to the processes exploring your issues like a duck takes to water'.

Pat's response was like a wake-up call. As I looked at the rich journey of my retreat, I realised what she said was true, but I had not joined the dots. Somewhere lodged within me was the memory of being told I was insensitive. I believed that I didn't have the sensitivity to become a counsellor. Yet as I thought about it, I realised that my work over the years had taken me into many situations that called for real sensitivity. As well as that, there were people who had sought me out to work with them at a deeper level.

A few months after this retreat would see the end of my current ministry. What would be next? Pat's suggestion that I do the training course was one possibility, but I would need to take time to discern whether I was called in that direction:

As I look back over my life, I can see that as far back as I remember, I have felt there was a lot locked up inside me that needs to see the light of day. I had no idea what it was. I used to pray, especially before and during retreats that the retreat leader would be able to help me talk about it. But neither I, nor the retreat director, had the skills and understanding for that work. 19.6.1995

I could see that what Pat offered could give me the skills I sought. I would also be able to accompany others seeking such help. But is this where the Spirit was leading me? Over the following weeks, I found a 'yes' forming within me – a 'yes' I recognised as the voice of the Spirit. I responded in the only way I could, and this was to take me into a whole new phase of my journey and my mission.

2
Opening a box of worms

When Pat first suggested to me to do the counselling training course, she told me it would give me 'a year to clear my stuff'. I wondered: Do I have that much 'stuff' that I need a year to clear it? I ended up doing a second year of training – and I still had not exhausted the lifetime of 'stuff' that welled up from deep within. The experiential processes took the lid off the box of worms of my unresolved issues. I discovered unconscious beliefs and assumptions that were holding me back. I touched into hidden fears, defensiveness, patterns of seeing and interpreting my everyday experiences, my need to control, and much more.

Each of us participants in the course had to face our own version of such things. Working through them opened unsuspected potential and energy which I had locked up with those aspects of myself I hadn't wanted to acknowledge. The course led me into an inner world that was vaster, richer, and more complex than I ever suspected. At the end of my graduate diploma year, I wrote the following reflection:

The Pearl Beyond Price

I've been on a journey these past two years:
  a journey exploring inner space,
  seeking, in secret depths,
  the Pearl of great price,
  the Divine
  at the core of my being.

Seeking, I found paradox;
  I experienced Mystery.

Something profound has changed:
  I know myself stronger
  in the midst of weaknesses
  I did not know before;
  I know myself more whole

and at the same time more broken and wounded;
I experience deep wisdom and insight,
yet know myself blind and foolish
to the simplest truths of my own being;
I am silenced in the face of my sacredness
while I see more clearly my sinfulness.

The umbilical cord
   tying me to the maternal womb,
   which has had me looking over my shoulder
   for 'mother's' approval,
   has been cut –
     I am more myself
     and know myself as part of a whole
     which encompasses All that is.
     I am able to stand alone
     precisely in the knowledge
     that I am deeply connected to Life itself.

My armour cracked,
   defences less secure,
   I am vulnerable, fearful,
   yet confident that nothing –
   neither pain nor misfortune,
   malevolent powers, even death
   can destroy the Divine at the core of my being.

This journey has been a grace
   for me and for the world.

Because of what has been
   I step into the future
   more grounded in the now,
   confident that my giftedness lies
   not in what I know,
   nor in what I can do,
   but in simply being who and what I am.

*I am learning to live
  in creative doubt,
  surrendering to a greater Wisdom
  at work in the journey,
  knowing there are times
  when the best I can do
  is not do.*

*And I am learning to listen
  with the whole of my being –
  my ears, my eyes,
  my heart, my spirit –
  present to myself,
  present to others,
  trusting the process,
  theirs and mine,
  each step revealed
  only as we take it.*

*There are doorways into the deep:
  dreams, memories, stories, body signals...*

*There are mirrors reflecting my truth:
  people and situations evoking energies and reactions...*

*There are processes and skills for the work:
  symbols, gestalts, journaling,
  drawing, bodywork, breathwork,
  dreamwork, music, meditation, imagination,
  voice and touch...*

*There is a time and timing
  which cannot be hurried,
  for the works of the psyche
  are beyond the laws of time.*

*I have experienced them all.
  Not that I have arrived:
  I am not yet finished.
  But this much is ready now.*

To know and be known

The time has come
　to take the reins of my life
　into my own hands,
　to set my own course,
　shape my own dream,
　create my own way,
　daring to envisage
　and be part of the movement
　toward a world made new,
　where all are welcomed and at home,
　because goodness and love
　so embrace injustice, violence and destruction
　that all is redeemed,
　made whole and wholesome,

and the Pearl Beyond Price
　reveals itself as
　the Divine at the core
　of each one's being.

For this vision to be fulfilled,
　I/we must live as though it were
　already fulfilled.　　　　　　　　3.5.1997

3
Until I see: awakening to the cosmos

My experience of the work at the Portiuncula greatly expanded my inner universe, opening resources I never suspected hidden in my own depths. But there was another moment that was to have a lasting impact on me.

I came into the Portiuncula kitchen one morning and found one of my fellow trainees at the table, reading while eating his breakfast. I asked him what he was reading. He showed me *The Tao of Physics* by Fritjof Capra.[21] As I looked at that book and saw what it was about, I knew it was something I simply *had* to read. In the opening paragraph of the Preface, Capra recounts an experience:

> I was sitting by the ocean one late summer afternoon, watching the waves rolling in and feeling the rhythm of my breathing, when I suddenly became aware of my whole environment as being engaged in a gigantic cosmic dance. Being a physicist, I knew that the sand, rocks, water and air around me were made of vibrating molecules and atoms... As I sat on that beach, ... I 'saw' cascades of energy coming from outer space... I 'saw' atoms of the elements and those of my body participating in this cosmic dance of energy; I felt its rhythm and 'heard' its sound, and at that moment I knew that this was the Dance of Shiva, the Lord of Dancers worshipped by the Hindus.

During his years of study and research in theoretical physics, Capra had become interested in Eastern mysticism. He saw that many of its core insights paralleled the discoveries and insights of modern

---

21 Fritjof Capra, *The Tao of Physics, Exploring the Parallels Between Modern Physics and Eastern Mysticism*, third edition, Flamingo 1993. The first edition was published in 1976.

physics. Experiences like the one recounted above, brought those parallels to life for him. It led him to write *The Tao of Physics*.

Capra awakened me to the Universe, to a Cosmos far more astonishing and mysterious than I ever suspected. Perhaps I understood only a fraction of what I read, not ever having studied physics, but it ignited a fire in my belly. In my journal I wrote:

> *I started to read Fritjof Capra's* The Tao of Physics *yesterday. As I read, I feel a sense of excitement in my belly, and a longing – for what? I suspect it has to do with the experience of the oneness of all things in the One. He writes of a mystical experience in which he saw everything as moving, dancing energy – 'the dance of Shiva', he called it. It reminded me of an experience on the rocks at Shark Point, in which the boundaries of all I saw around me seemed to dissolve. I 'saw' something of its inner reality, and I was part of it, in continuity with it. I experienced a profound silence in the heart of being. I was lost in the immensity of it, yet fully aware. Or maybe I was truly found in that immensity.* 14.8.1996

Astounded by what I discovered in that book, I realised it had implications for every field of life and knowledge, including philosophy, theology and spirituality, as well as for the way we live and relate to one another and to all other beings. I wondered, why did none of this come into the lectures during my theology course? How come today's theologians are not exploring this astonishing revelation coming through science? I knew I had to do my theology all over again – a daunting task.

Of course, there *were* theologians who had begun to explore the meaning and implications of what was being discovered by science. Years earlier, I had read Teilhard de Chardin's *Hymn of the Universe*[22] and was drawn to his mystical vision of matter. I had read Matthew

---

22 Pierre Teilhard de Chardin, *Hymn of the Universe*, Collins Fountain Books 1977, English version first published in 1965.

Fox's *Original Blessings*[23] and learned to appreciate creation in a new and deeper way. I had read Denis Edwards' *Jesus and the Cosmos*.[24] Women theologians, such as Sally McFague, Rosemary Radford Reuther and Elizabeth Johnson were at the forefront of the new frontier of theology, exploring the interface of science and religion. I had read some of their works, and my journals record a growing awareness of our amazing Universe. But only when I read *The Tao of Physics* did the cosmic story become real and personal for me.

I have come to realise that *I cannot see what I cannot see until I see*! It took a physicist to bring into full focus what had been growing in me. Capra opened my vision to the vitality of the Cosmos, and I caught a glimpse of something so vast, so mysterious, so exciting and amazing, I was smitten! Until then, creation as a process of evolution was something I was only vaguely aware of. Now it became a living reality. It impacted on me with an immediacy I never anticipated. In the years since, I have not stopped exploring and pondering the amazing process of creation, which wasn't finished on the sixth day, as the first chapter of Genesis says. It has been in the process of becoming for almost fourteen billion years and still isn't finished!

My awakening to the Cosmos gradually began to dissolve the boundaries of my individual world. Perhaps the first seeds of what I came to see were sown during that retreat at John Fisher College in 1978, when I heard, 'The Word was made flesh, and her name is Corrie'. That moment set me on a life-long journey of pondering the mystery of the Incarnation: Everything that is, is a Word of God become creation. Now I caught a glimpse of the entire creation as one vast being, consisting of countless individual beings, each of which plays its part in the great ongoing creative process of the Cosmos coming into Being. The entire process is the Word of God become – becoming – creation. Life is not about me as an individual, but about me as one infinitesimal part of the Whole. That does not make us individual beings insignificant. Everything that exists is called to play

---

23 Matthew Fox, *Original Blessings: a Primer in Creation Spirituality*, Bear & Co, Sante Fe, New Mexico, 1983. The book is still in print.
24 Denis Edwards, *Jesus and the Cosmos*, St Paul Publications 1991. Edwards spent decades of his life exploring the theological and spiritual implications of the discoveries of science.

its part in the Cosmic Becoming. The *Tao of Physics* drew me into what I now know as cosmology, or, as Teilhard de Chardin named it, cosmogenesis.

A Universe so vast, amazing and mysterious, challenged my inherited ways of seeing my everyday world, and also my thinking about God and Christ. I hungered to learn more. Around the time I was reading Capra, Diarmuid O'Murchu msc[25] was publishing his *Quantum Theology* and *Reclaiming Spirituality*. These were the first books I read after my initial awakening to the Cosmos. Over the years since, many theologians and mystics, working at the intersection of ancient wisdom traditions and the discoveries of modern science, have given birth to very rich and fertile theologies. Turning to mystics of East and West, they discovered that the mystical intuition had long seen what modern science is discovering today. I suspect it is only mystical experience that enables us to embody cosmogenesis as a lived reality.

There is an urgent need for humans to grow into cosmic evolutionary consciousness. Our modern way of life has led to a crisis point in which Earth and its life-systems are under grave threat. While authorities are slow to take action, more and more people are speaking out for the Earth, their voices growing stronger and more urgent with each passing year. Our young people are at the forefront of this movement.

Genuine cosmic consciousness awakens a profound love and awe for the Cosmos and for everything that makes up the Cosmos. Without such love there can be no effective action, no long-term commitment to caring for our small portion of it. As the environmentalist, Baba Dioum, said many decades ago: 'In the end we will conserve only what we love'.[26]

---

25 O'Murchu has published many books around these topics, his latest *Doing Theology in an Evolutionary Way*, published February 2021. https://diarmuidomurchu.com/
26 The full quote reads, 'In the end we will conserve only what we love. We love only what we understand. We will understand only what we are taught'. It comes from a talk Baba Dioum gave to the 1968 General Assembly of the International Union for the Conservation of Nature.

As I read through my journals, I notice that the influence of the cosmic story begins to permeate my consciousness more and more. Pondering a decision I had to make, I wrote:

> *In a way, these are small matters. I sense I am living on the threshold of stupendous mystery. Or am I enveloped by it? Maybe my questions and feelings are part of it too. They fit somewhere in the cosmic mosaic which is God's self-expression. There, big and small, significance or insignificance are very relative. The Universe is no vaster for a tiny meat ant than it is for me, though I marvel that something so small can have limbs and organs almost smaller than my eye can see.*

Twenty-five years on from *The Tao of Physics*, I continue to grow into this cosmogenic Mystery. It is a story we need to tell over and over again, until we grow into it and it becomes central to our sense of who we are. It is *our* story, the story of every creature. The entire universe is kin. Our Indigenous brothers and sisters have always known this. The elements that make up all living beings were birthed in generations of dying stars. As Brian Swimme says, it took fourteen billion years of evolution for us to be here. Our human part in the story is so critical that the future of our Earth depends on it, for better or for worse. For better, if we consciously take up our responsibility of caring for the Earth, for all living beings and for the environment that sustains us. If we remain mindless about it, we may well be in the process of writing the last chapter of the Earth's ability to sustain life.

4
Expanding consciousness

In 1996, I participated in a two-week workshop in Grof Transpersonal Training[27] (GTT), exploring the healing potential of non-ordinary states of consciousness and holotropic breathwork. The course took place in Maleny, in a conference centre built on top of a ridge overlooking the beautiful Glasshouse Mountains, mountains sacred to the Aboriginal people.

One of Stan Grof's core insights is that consciousness does not reside in the human brain. It doesn't come from us at all. Rather, Grof recognises consciousness as a cosmic reality in which every being participates, whether aware of this or not. If this is so, it opens a further window on my growing realisation that we are interconnected with everything that is.

Over the years since, I have continued to ponder the mystery of consciousness: What is it? What does it mean to be conscious? How do I know, and know that I know? And, as ancient Upanishad sages ask: Who is the knower in me?

Some physicists are posing the possibility that consciousness may be that from which the Cosmos itself arises, that it is a field that envelopes all that exists.[28] Could this actually be what we mean by the Cosmic Christ? There is so much to wonder about, taking me ever deeper into the mystery of Being itself.

I began to see that, if consciousness is what gives birth to the Cosmos, my own consciousness creates my world. It shapes what and how I see and interpret what is happening in my life and in the world. And our collective human consciousness has shaped the world we live in.

---

27 Stanislav Grof is a Czech psychiatrist who has spent his life exploring human states of consciousness and the healing potential of non-ordinary states of consciousness. The breathwork of our TEP training was based on Stan's work. At the time of writing, he is approaching his 90th birthday, and still teaching and writing.
28 E.g. Ervin Laszlo, *Science and the Askashic Field, An Integral Theory of Everything*, downloadable as a pdf from the internet.

> *There are enormous issues in our world – even to the survival of life on the planet. Can my life and work contribute to bringing about a healthy change? Everything I do, think and feel makes a difference, for better or for worse. The more I live each moment consciously and help others to do the same, the more globally will human consciousness be affected. And if anything is going to change globally, it is going to come through a change in our collective human consciousness. We can dismantle institutions, but without a change in consciousness we will simply rebuild them under a different guise.* 14.5.1998

Our times are experiencing great and violent dysfunction in our world: oppression, poverty, wars, devastating climate events, excessive wealth, power and control in the hands of a few people and corporations. The list goes on and on. Christopher Fry, in his poem, *A Sleep of Prisoners*, speaks to me about what all this dysfunction might mean:

> The human heart can go the lengths of God.
> Dark and cold we may be, but this
> Is no winter now. The frozen misery
> Of centuries breaks, cracks, begins to move;
> The thunder is the thunder of the floes,
> The thaw, the flood, the upstart spring.
>
> Thank God our time is now, when wrong
> Comes up to face us everywhere
> Never to leave us till we take
> The longest stride of soul men ever took.
> Affairs are now soul size.
> The enterprise
> Is exploration into God.
> Where are you making for? It takes
> So many thousand years to wake,
> But will you wake for pity's sake![29]

---

[29] Christopher Fry, *A Sleep of Prisoners*, a verse play published by Geoffrey Cumberlege, Oxford University Press, London 1951.

All these years later, I still go back to this poem and its profound realisation that our growing consciousness of the ills of our world is calling us to face up to the wrongs of our world, including the wrongs of human history. The poem challenges us to dare face our larger reality: *Affairs of life are soul size now. The enterprise is exploration into God.* My own spiritual journey, my life-long exploration into God, is not only deeply meaningful for me: the ills of our world demand that we do this collectively.

5
A spark of the Divine

If I thought that, during those two years of counselling training, working through 'all my stuff' would rid me of my self-centred and defensive inclinations, I couldn't have been more wrong. I continue to meet 'my stuff' in its numerous manifestations, and the pain and struggle that accompanies it. Of course, I would like to be healed of my ego's life-long habits:

> *Yesterday's Gospel was about the woman who for eighteen years had been bent double because of an evil spirit. Maybe I too can be healed of my ego spirit this time round, and surrender what I want and don't want so I can be truly free.*
>
> *As I write this, I find myself with the question – free for what? Perhaps my desire for freedom of heart is really a desire not to feel pain. Perhaps the freedom is not so much to be rid of my ego or my shadow, but to accept myself as I am, with all that entails – my weakness, sinfulness, and the pain that is inevitably part of life – to surrender to the moments and forces that are shaping me – not as a helpless victim but as an active participant.* 27.10.1998

I was learning to accept that I am a wounded human being, alongside every other human being, each of us carrying our own wounds. More than that, I came to appreciate that it is precisely my wounds which have opened the way to my growth. Suffering revealed itself to me as grace. For that grace to take root in me and bring about the transformation it offers, I needed to accept my vulnerability, to lean into the pain and discomfort. For too long I built and maintained defences around that vulnerability. But as I learned to accept it and become at home in it, I discovered its grace. I began to realise that I didn't have to be perfect in order to be loveable.

Life is not about perfection, but about living each moment as it is, the light and the dark, the joy and the pain, the groping in the mists of confusion and not-knowing and the delight of moments of clarity. I came to realise that, at heart, the spiritual journey is about surrendering to what is, in body, mind and spirit. This is the only way to enter that inner freedom I always longed for.

It seems to me that the word spirituality itself was problematic for me. I understood it as referring to my relationship with God, a God who was elsewhere. I asked myself:

> *What is spirituality? I run courses exploring spirituality – and don't know how to live my own spiritual life! I spend time, intentionally for prayer. Yet I am anywhere except what looks like prayer. What has happened to my relationship with God? with Jesus? I have less of sense of who they are in my life than I have ever had. I long, I thirst, and always more so. At the same time, I experience a deep inner peace and joy. Perhaps the whole spiritual life is about surrender – letting go of anything and everything that might suggest I am growing spiritually, in communion with God and the Universe. And to surrender even the desire to surrender. What is is, regardless of how I experience or perceive it. The Divine permeates everything as the ocean permeates the salt.* 11.8.1998

I was still learning that spirituality is not about what I experience in prayer. It is about how I live my life in the ordinary every day. It is about how I relate and respond to people and situations, for that is where the Christ-mystery becomes real among us.

> *In my growing up years, I dreamt of being a saint. Now I know I am one – but not in the way I understood back then. I know I am holy because all that is is sacred, is God's self-expression. This is so for saint and sinner alike. It doesn't depend on what I do or how I am. I simply long, and live that longing peacefully yet restlessly, yet confidently – knowing that Christ Jesus has grasped hold of my heart irrevocably...* 15.8.1998

During a session on pastoral care, I invited participants to name the gift they bring to their work. Reflecting on this question for myself:

> *One gift I bring is an appreciation of the sacred in the ordinary, the wonder and mystery that lies within the simplest things, gestures, incidents. I guess that's what touched people today. The process enabled them to experience it too, recognising what they already knew, the gift of seeing the extraordinary in the ordinary.*
> 24-25.10.1998

In my counselling practice, I encountered the extraordinary in the ordinary again and again. Many of the people who sought counselling had tragic stories of abuse, often experienced during their childhood and adolescence. Many managed to block out the memory of their traumas. But there comes a time in life when traumas of the past well up from deep within, bringing the bearer close to breaking point.

Again and again, as people worked through their experiences, I saw, beneath all that brokenness, something at the core of their being that was totally uncontaminated, unspoilt by their experiences. I met a purity, an innocence, and a beauty that I recognise as a spark of the Divine within that person. It reminded me of what my father told me about his orchids. When an orchid became diseased by a virus, he would slice off a new growth tip and send it away for tissue culture. The plant that developed from this was always healthy, because – he told me – a growth tip is always healthy, even when its parent is diseased. So with us. There is a Divine spark at the core of our being. Once a person touches this centre in him or herself, even though they may not be able to name it, something new happens in them, setting them on their journey towards healing. The scars of the wounds may remain, but the person no longer identifies with them.

It takes patient trust and consistent inner work to clear the window to our inner vision and see our real beauty. In my counselling practice, I often wished, in the beautiful words of the Sufi poet Hafiz,

> I wish I could show you,
> When you are lonely or in darkness,
> The Astonishing Light
> Of your own Being![30]

---

30 From the poem, My Brilliant Image, Daniel Ladinsky, *I Heard God Laughing: Renderings of Hafiz*, Sufism Reoriented, California, 1996, p. 13.

That Astonishing Light, that Spark of the Divine, lives at the heart of every created being. It is that deep Wisdom which guides the creative process of our evolutionary Universe from within. It is in all living beings. Animals in the wild, when unwell, instinctively seek out plants with the properties they need for their healing. Some of today's farmers are discovering that the Earth also has a Wisdom which guides its healing where it is out of balance or depleted. Indigenous peoples have always been attuned to this, living in their environment with all their senses open and receptive. It needs a heart that loves and reverences the land and all that lives and grows there. When we learn to cooperate with nature's ways, nature begins to restore itself, bringing renewed flourishing to depleted soils and natural biodiversities.[31] Such attunement and cooperation is critical, both for our own wellbeing and that of the Earth.

There is a consistency throughout all levels of creation. It requires us to look and see with the eye of the heart, with the eye of love. When we do, we meet the within-ness[32] of creation. We encounter that Sacred Presence, just as I did time and time again in the people who came for counselling. It is also what I experienced in the vast solitude of the Hay Plains or in moments like that day on Shark Point, where I knew myself embraced and held by Love in the presence of Astonishing Mystery, a Presence both deeply personal and infinitely more than personal – the Unnameable One we call God.

---

31 See e.g. Charles Massey, *The Call of the Reed Warbler: A New Agriculture, A New Earth*, University of Queensland Press, Revised Edition, 2020. Also Victor Steffensen's *Fire Country: How Indigenous Fire Management Could Help Save Australia*, Hardy Travel Publishing, 2020.
32 Teilhard de Chardin sj, scientist and palaeontologist used the term *the within of matter*, which is where he encountered the presence of Christ. Another way he expressed this was to see matter on fire with the Divine Presence.

6
Feed them with your flesh

'I listen to God speaking...' (Psalm 85:8): It is only in deep listening, in contemplation, that we hear the vision of God for the Universe and for our place in it individually and as a people. But deep listening isn't easy. It involves going beyond my ego-driven self, open to having my understanding stretched, challenged, perhaps even shattered. It involves letting go of the entanglements and ownerships of my heart, of material and immaterial things such as ideas, status, reputation or whatever...
15.5.1999

Such listening takes me to my place in the Universe, not as something separate from the Universe, but as integrally part of it, as organs are part of an organism, everything interdependent with everything else. I longed to realise this more and more, and to help others to realise it. Yet, how could I share this with them?

Whenever I set myself to prepare a course or a session, I found a blank emptiness within. As the time for the session drew nearer, a panicky feeling would rise up within me. In my journal, I wrote about this experience, searching out what was blocking me.

It isn't like preparing a meal for a group. It is more like feeding them from my flesh. I can only present effectively what I know from my own experience.   22.6.1999

Feed them with my flesh. Coming onto this expression in my journal took me by surprise. It is audaciously Eucharistic. I don't know that I fully appreciated the meaning of that statement at the time. But all these years later, I see it is not only audacious, it is at the heart of what it is to live the Eucharist. In the Eucharist, we share the Body and Blood of Christ in forms of bread and wine, a holy communion. In that communion, we become the Body of Christ. It is to become what Jesus was, to live as he lived, and to give ourselves as he did, as food for the hungry, for the hungers of the human heart.

Through these years, I came to realise that there is an inner Wisdom that can guide us on our healing journey. As counsellor, I need to listen for that Wisdom in my client and create the space in which the client can do the same. As I listen deeply to the other, I am also listening to the Spirit present in that encounter, guiding us both in what the person needs in that moment. At times, I was surprised by my spontaneous response to the client's process, hearing myself say things I did not realise I knew, and it always was right for that moment. There is a profound sacredness in this work.

While my counselling practice sensitised me to individual people's suffering, my journals also tell of my growing consciousness of suffering wherever it happens in the world. Sometimes I despair at the dysfunction and violence in human relationships, whether on an interpersonal level or an interethnic or international level:

> *The belief of a fallen human creation needing redemption fits what I see in the human world – greed, violence, oppression, war, crime. We do need redemption, but not from an original sin committed by an original ancestor. We need to re-find ourselves in relationship with every creature. We need to find ourselves at home, not in an out-there spiritual place we call heaven after we die, but here, in harmony with every other creature. When we do find it and live it, we are concerned, not merely with our individual redemption, not even that of the human species, but of Earth as a whole and ourselves as part of the whole.* 21.3.1999

Over the years, the suffering of the world has worked its way more deeply into my heart. During Holy Week 1999, the war in Kosovo was constantly in the news:

> *How many Good Fridays does it take before we learn that no war brings redemption? that every child born into this world is a child of the Universe and therefore has a right to be here? that we cannot claim exclusive possession over any area of Earth, whether individually or ethnically or nationally? that no one has the right to have more*

> *than they need while others have less than they need and while the needs of other-than-human living beings are disregarded? Do we human beings need to die out for the Earth to survive as a living planet? It is in the awareness of the pain and despair of this world that I need the hope of resurrection.*   4.4.1999

Again and again through my life, I ponder the mystery of suffering. As I mentioned earlier, suffering has revealed itself to me as grace. There can be no growth without suffering. Nor can we experience real joy if we avoid suffering. I have often been amazed in times of deep inner suffering that I simultaneously experienced deep joy. Thich Nhat Hahn says, 'Joy and suffering inter-are'. They are two sides of the one reality that is life, just as darkness and light are part of the cycle of day and night.

This does not imply that I have to seek out suffering. Rather, suffering seeks me out, often in the most unexpected moments. It catches me out, holding up a mirror to my inner life, my shadow, my blind spots. It shows me that the source of my suffering is within myself. Until I can see that, I will tend to see it in another, blaming him or her. When I turn that mirror to face myself, it shows me where I need healing and conversion. It took many years before I really understood this, but as its truth dawned on me, it awakened my capacity for understanding, patience and compassion – for myself as well as for others.

The suffering of others calls me to open my heart to them and to stand up against the gratuitous suffering we human beings continue to visit on one another and on the Earth. It calls me to see that the potential to such violence is also in me. When I become aware of this, I can choose to act otherwise. I can respond in love to both perpetrators and victims of violence. Part of such love and compassion is naming the wrongs, particularly of the systems that create or elicit violence and the cultural stories behind these systems. Such love is a grace. It is the love with which God loves me, that desires to flow through me to every neighbour, human and other-than-human, including Earth itself, just as God's love comes to me through them. This also is feeding them with my flesh.

God's love is like blood coursing through the vascular system of the Universe, bringing life and nourishment to the whole and to each part, no matter how small or insignificant it might seem. Am I an open capillary in that bloodstream, enabling love to flow through to the rest of the body?

Part VI

A new millennium

1
Dispossession

The jubilee year has begun with fireworks and celebrations around the globe. In a fantastic feat of co-operation, we received 24 hours of telecasts, showing, in place after place, the celebrations as midnight struck. What a welcome change from the gloom, doom, wars and violence that usually fill the news bulletins! If we can co-operate for an occasion like this, surely we can do it for the rest of the century. But for that, we must live the spirit of jubilee: forgiving debt, freeing prisoners, bringing justice to the oppressed, sharing our wealth with the poor. 3.1.2000

The turn of the millennium brought to a close the most violent century our world has seen, and ushered in the hope of a new start, a new era. But it wasn't long before the world realised that we continue to live with the reality of our wounded humanity.

I ask myself: What has characterised the opening years of the New Millennium in my experience? The question brings to mind a mandala that I drew in 2000. I titled it Dispossession. At many levels I found myself challenged to let go, to be detached from things, from outcomes, from my securities and certainties. I ask:
Is it possible to live in total detachment, yet with passion and compassion?
Is it possible to experience true freedom in which status, security, acceptability, etc. no longer bind me to certain behaviours? 8.6.2002

Detachment, freedom of heart, is a journey. When it concerns a matter close to my heart, I find it a searing process. The irony is, that once I really let go of whatever I cling to, I wonder why I found it such a big deal!

One day during my meditation a question arose within me:

> *Who am I if I am not a Catholic, not a Missionary Sister of Service, not a counsellor, not a van den Bosch, Australian or Dutch, nor any of the other ways I might use to identify myself? Who would I be if I walked out of this place, leaving all of that behind?*   6.5.2005

As I stripped off, one by one, all the accidentals of my personhood, I found myself on the precipice of an unfathomable void: I am Nothing. Yet that Nothingness holds an amazing richness. It is an experience of mystery vastly greater than my inner mystery. Its reach and source are the very Mystery of the Divine.

Reflecting on this, I smile: I remember how, several decades earlier, I was terrified of getting to know my inner self: What if I found nothing there? Now I know that there really is Nothing there: my inner being is total Nothingness, a rich, beautiful, empty, dark, fathomless Nothingness. Yet that Nothingness holds everything that is!

Every letting go is a kind of dying. The pattern is at the heart of the Divine Mystery, so tellingly expressed in the hymn in Paul's letter to the Philippians:

> Let the same mind be in you as was also in Christ Jesus,
> Who, being in the form of God,
> did not count equality with God
> something to be grasped.
> But he emptied himself,
> taking the form of a slave,
> becoming as human beings are;
> and being in every way a human being,
> he humbled himself,
> becoming obedient unto death,
> death on a cross.
>
> Philippians 2:5-8

As I continue to ponder this mystery, I see that such letting go is an act of unconditional self-giving love. It is the pattern built into every aspect of creation from the very beginning.

A journal entry written on the last Christmas of the twentieth century reads:

> *The Word was made Flesh and dwelt among us. The Mystery we celebrate is not just of a moment in history, 2000 years ago. It is the Mystery of our God, unfolding in ever new ways from the dawn of creation until now – and continuing forever. It is a call to move beyond life and death, into the mystery of BEING itself. The Word made Flesh remains the Word even when the flesh has to be surrendered. Every birth involves a death and every death a new birth, for nothing ceases to exist. All is transformed. My life, my being, is less than the blink of an eye in the context of the whole mystery of Being. Yet what an amazingly wonderful blink!* 25.12.1999

On the eve of the new millennium I was asked, 'What do you want to leave behind as we enter the new millennium?' My spontaneous response was 'my fears'. It seemed to me that, if the whole human community could leave its fears behind, we would have a world without violence. But, of course, that is too simplistic. Fears are part of life. What I need to learn is to not let them paralyse me. Rather, gather my courage and do what I know I need to do, even to allowing myself to be stripped naked. Paradoxically, there is deep joy in this nakedness, the fruit of love that lets go of fear.

While my journal records a growing awareness of this all-encompassing reality, it also shows how I had to learn its lessons over and over again. Several years later, again during meditation, a question dropped into my mind: What if I were to walk out of the gate naked? Instantly I was filled with terror. All my survival instincts rushed to the fore: How would I keep warm? Where would I sleep? How would I survive? The question remained with me. I couldn't shake it off. Reflecting on it, I came to see that walking naked is about letting go, not only of attachments to things or situations or desires, but also letting go of the armour with which I protect my vulnerability.

A new millennium

Walking naked is the invitation to let myself to be stripped down to the bare reality of who I am, to stand naked, like the tree of my mandala, vulnerable to the rough and tumble of life. It is the way of paradox, which T. S. Eliot expresses powerfully in his poem:

> ... In order to arrive there
> To arrive where you are, to get from where you are not,
> You must go by a way wherein there is no ecstasy.
> In order to arrive at what you do not know
> You must go by a way which is the way of ignorance.
> In order to possess what you do not possess
> You must go by the way of dispossession
> In order to arrive at what you are not
> You must go through the way in which you are not...
> And what you do not know is the only thing you know
> And what you own is the only thing you do not own
> And where you are is where you are not.
> – from *East Coker*[33]

As I ponder the core of the Christ Mystery in the world in which I live and move and have my being, I realise more and more that I am integrally part of Something much larger than myself. I am part of the body which is the Cosmos which is the Body of God. Everything I do, value, think and live, impacts on the whole Body. This awareness is not evident in today's world and the stories that inform it. But there is an awakening happening: I learn of more and more people who are growing into this wider consciousness and try to live accordingly.

Our world still runs on the supreme value of individualism. Individual freedom and rights are frequently invoked to justify individual demands. But I wonder: are we as conscious of the social responsibilities that circumscribe our individual rights and freedoms? At its core, our problem is our collective ignorance of our true place in the world, of our being part of the body of humanity, of the Earth and beyond that, of the Cosmos. Our rights and freedoms are circumscribed by what serves the good of the entire body. For that, I need to let go my privileges, at least until those same privileges are afforded to everyone, including our natural environment.

A final word on letting go:

---

[33] http://www.davidgorman.com/4quartets/2-coker.htm

Love with all your being – and let go that which you love!
Impossible? Nothing is impossible with God.   19.7.2001

Detachment, letting go, walking naked, is a grace, and I have been abundantly graced again and again – and not without tears!

2
The healing power of forgiveness

Many of the people who came to me for counselling had suffered abuse of various kinds early in life. Not infrequently, they blamed themselves for what happened to them. When I pointed out that the abuse wasn't their fault, they would often say, 'I must have done something to deserve it'. That deeply embedded belief made it difficult for the person to see the abuse for what it really is and to begin the healing process.

Victims of abuse have to deal with many layers of their experience and reactions. If it happened during childhood, they usually suppressed all memories of it. This is a survival mechanism for the child. But the experience remains embedded in their psyche and affects their lives. At some stage, the memories emerge and throw the person into crisis. It takes enormous courage to confront the reality of what was done to them. She/he has to deal with the anger and rage, the sense of powerlessness, loss of innocence and grief. As their therapist, I have to hold the space for them as, bit by bit, they feel safe enough to let those feelings come to consciousness and to express them in that protected space.

I don't have ready answers for people in that situation. Each person and their story is unique. As I reflect back on my years of practice, I 'hear' within myself the words of Miriam Rose Ungunmerr-Baumann:

> To know me is to breathe with me
> To breathe with me is to listen deeply
> To listen deeply is to connect...[34]

Again and again, I would ask the client to become aware of their breath: to breathe and notice whatever within them was coming to their attention. And I would breathe with them, listening deeply, waiting for whatever would arise within myself as well as in the other.

---

[34] Miriam Rose Ungunmerr-Baumann, *Dadirri*. The words are taken from the short YouTube by that title, https://www.youtube.com/watch?v=tow2tR_ezL8.

It often takes many sessions to peel back the layers of fear, rage, pain and grief in their many guises. If they can stay the course, there comes a moment when they can stand sufficiently aside from those experiences to recognise that they are more than their experience of abuse and all its consequences. At that stage, the person needs to look at forgiveness: forgiving themselves when they have blamed themselves for that abuse, and forgiving the abuser. But the mere mention of forgiveness can bring up another level of anger: 'I couldn't. That's like telling them that what they did was alright'. I would respond something like:

> *Forgiveness is <u>not</u> saying what happened is alright. It can <u>never</u> be alright. Forgiveness is about stepping out of the shackles that have kept you bound to the abuser all these years, though the perpetrator hasn't been in your life for a long time. In a way, the abuse continues while those shackles bind you.*

I would tell them that they need to find within themselves a desire to step out of those shackles. Only then can a person begin the journey to forgiveness. I can only point out the direction where healing can be found, and tell them that, when they feel ready, I will support them to find that heart-place in which they can forgive. And I would suggest they pray for that grace, or, if the person could not pray, to connect with their Higher Power, as they say in Alcoholics Anonymous.

On a number of occasions, clients told me that they felt possessed by a demonic presence. Such possibility called me to deep discernment: could this really be the case? And if so, what am I called to do about it? In one such case, there was no time to discern. Some strange entity reacted furiously when the woman told me she was ready to forgive her abuser. Guided by what the Gospels said about how Jesus dealt with evil spirits, I kept telling it to go back to where it belonged and prayed the familiar prayers and hymns that are part of the rich treasury of our Catholic tradition. The strongest reactions came to any mention of God's mercy and forgiveness.

The woman asked to have a Mass of forgiveness celebrated by the leader of the order of the priest who had abused her. It was two weeks before this could take place. During those weeks that demonic entity frequently tormented her. The amazing part of the experience for me was that, while I was with the woman during those attacks, I was calm and confident. I experienced an inner strength guiding me in my response. Outside those times, I felt shaken and a deep weariness. I sought people who I thought could support and guide me, but none of those I contacted had had such experience. To be with that women day after day in that supportive role was exhausting.

At last the day arrived when we could celebrate the Eucharist with her. The priest arrived and we sat at the kitchen bench for a chat and a cuppa. The entity attacked again, throwing the woman backwards onto the floor, screaming. We carried her into the prayer room and began the liturgy. She screamed all the way through, until we came to the Our Father. Then a peace came over her and silence descended in the room. When the priest gave her Communion, she offered the host back to him, asking him to break it with her. They consumed together.

Afterwards, she told us that she saw the face of her abuser in the face of the priest. Asking him to break the host with her was a profound act, signifying her forgiveness: consuming the Body of Christ together, she was now at–one with the man who had caused her so much suffering.

Two days later, I began my annual retreat. The timing, although arranged months earlier, couldn't have been more providential. I needed time to rest and ponder the experience of the previous weeks and months. It left me with an overwhelming sense of the power of forgiveness to heal, not only the one who forgives, but also the one she forgives. I realised, in a way I had not seen before, that forgiveness is the heart and core of the Good News and of Jesus' own life, even to his praying for forgiveness for those who crucified him. Forgiveness should also be at the heart of the Church in its life and mission, and in each one of us who bear the name Christian.

I drew several mandalas during that retreat. The act of drawing is a form of deep meditation, enabling me to enter my experience at a deeper level. I entitled this one, *The Fire and the Rose are One*.[35] For the woman of this story, the roses she placed on her former abuser's grave signified the transformation of her suffering into forgiveness.

What did I need to learn from this experience? I asked myself:

Do I still carry unforgiveness in my heart? Is there anyone with whom I am still angry or who I have walked away from and, because I am no longer with them, I have forgotten and not forgiven? I may not consciously hold anything against them now, but perhaps I need to specifically forgive. It is not enough to let time and distance cause the experience to fade. Forgiveness doesn't happen by default. It is a deliberate act.   19.11.2000

I also reflected on my thinking about the reality of the demonic. During the weeks we battled with it, I had written:

I am aware of my arrogance in taking an agnostic stance towards the powers of darkness. I have been very aware of the dark side of humanity and see it acted out in myriad ways in the world. And I know that I am part of that. But I had not allowed for the place of the powers of darkness in this. I am being shaken awake to this reality.   11.11.2000

---

35 The title comes from T. S. Eliott's *Four Quartets, Little Gidding*: And all shall be well and / All manner of thing shall be well / When the tongues of flame are in-folded / Into the crowned knot of fire / And the fire and the rose are one.

All these years later, I am surprised at how immediate my memories of this experience remain, though I have not thought about them for years. As T. S. Eliot's poem says:

> Now, we come to discover that moments of agony
> . . . are likewise permanent
> With such permanence as time has. We appreciate this better
> In the agony of others, nearly experienced,
> Involving ourselves, than in our own.
> For our own past is covered by currents of action,
> But the torment of others remains an experience
> Unqualified, unworn by subsequent attrition.
> The Dry Salvages[36]

Reflecting on this encounter with the demonic, I became aware of the support I drew from my Catholic heritage and my being part of the Body which is the Church:

Joining my prayer with people praying the world over, drawing on the faith of people and time-honoured prayers – all this was present for us in the fight against the dark power. I reflect on my attitude to the Church and know it has been ambivalent at best. I am estranged from the institution and the hierarchy that represents the institutional dimension of the Church. And yet – I am integrally a member of this body. It is the faith of the Church that enabled me to journey with this woman.

Commenting on another mandala which I entitled Dark Light:

I observe (N..'s) journey and see dark mysticism. I look at my own, and I can't see where I am. I see nothing, feel nothing, touch and taste nothing. I am not in the light. I am not in the dark. I do not have a sense of faith, hope or love. And yet, how could I live as I do, without these?

---

36 http://www.davidgorman.com/4quartets/3-salvages.htm

> *The fruits of the Spirit are there and, in all the absence of any sensible Presence, I am at peace. One thing I know: at the Voice of the Spirit, I would abandon everything I hold dear. This is a time of self-emptying.*   21.11.2000

Reading this entry today, I turn again to the poetry of T. S. Eliot. He speaks powerfully to my experience, sending a beam of light on its deeper meaning:

> I said to my soul, be still, and wait without hope
> For hope would be hope for the wrong thing; wait without love,
> For love would be love of the wrong thing; there is yet faith
> But the faith and the love and the hope are all in the waiting.
> Wait without thought, for you are not ready for thought:
> So the darkness shall be the light, and the stillness the dancing.
> Whisper of running streams, and winter lightning.
> The wild thyme unseen and the wild strawberry,
> The laughter in the garden, echoed ecstasy
> Not lost, but requiring, pointing to the agony
> Of death and birth.
>
>   *East Coker*[37]

Reflecting on encounters with the demonic, I once again find myself with the mystery of evil: what *are* the dark powers that dog our societies and individual people? Could it be that demons are actually our collective projections, blaming our 'evil' on a being who is not 'us'?

I turn to an insight of Teilhard de Chardin, that prophetic Jesuit, scientist and mystic. He posed that beyond the biosphere there is a *noosphere*[38] which envelopes the Earth. It consists of the cumulative

---

[37] http://www.davidgorman.com/4quartets/2-coker.htm
[38] Ursula King, *Spirit of Fire: The Life and Vision of Teilhard de Chardin*, Obis Books, NY, 1996, pp. 88-89.

consciousness of humanity from our beginnings and continues to develop with every human being's consciousness. If that is so, could it be that the evil we humans perpetrate has a place in the noosphere?

We humans create systems, some of which become so large and powerful that they seem to take on a life of their own. We can no longer control or dismantle them without huge destructive consequences. Could this also be the case with our collective evil? Has its accumulation in the noosphere become so powerful that it has taken on a life of its own? Could it be that this collective evil can manifest as an alien entity?

I am well out of my depth when raising such questions. But my experience with the dark powers taught me that deep healing only comes through forgiveness. Only forgiveness can release us from the shackles that keep us bound to those who wounded us. The wounding will always remain part of us, just as the risen Christ carries the wounds of the Crucified Jesus. But the wounds no longer hold us bound in a destructive dynamic. The act of forgiving transforms us and sets us free, and in the same movement sets the other free – whether the other knows it or not. Truly, forgiveness is a most profound grace, and only grace can enable us to forgive.

3
The priceless pearl

2002 marked the fortieth anniversary of my profession of vows. Looking back on those forty years, I was astonished at where the journey had taken me, and the transformation it had worked in me. I wanted to do something to honour the gift of my calling as a Missionary Sister of Service.

I have always been drawn to the parable of the pearl. A pearl is such a beautiful lustrous jewel. Yet it starts off as an irritation in the shell of an oyster. Instead of washing the grain of sand out of its shell, the oyster weaves a pearl around it, transforming it into something beautiful and precious. It seemed to me the perfect symbol for the extraordinary journey of those forty years, its joys and griefs, its challenges and its rich rewards. Like the grain of sand in the oyster's shell, the years had brought me many 'irritations', painful experiences and events. Yet, looking back on them, I could see that it was precisely these 'irritations' that caused me to grow beyond my very limited and limiting egoic world into the amazing mystery of life which I share with people, nature, the Cosmos, all within the astonishing Mystery we call God and by a thousand other names.

I took my worn and discoloured congregational symbol to a local jeweller and asked him could he make me one in sterling silver and, on the reverse side, put a pearl in a spiral. He said, 'Yes, I can do that, but it will cost you'. I replied, 'I know, and that's the idea of it'. He gave me a funny look. It was probably the most surprising response he had ever received. I told him the parable and the reason I decided to do what I had asked. I'm not sure that he understood, but he agreed to do what I asked, quoting me the price. Two months later:

> *The day before yesterday I picked up from the jeweller my pearl set in the reverse side of my MSS symbol. As I wear it, I find myself centering on its meaning – its quiet lustre awakening, or reawakening, my appreciation and gratitude for the gift of my calling into BEing, into my family, the Church and the MSS community and all that has come to me over the forty years since my profession. Its design is utterly simple and unpretentious, yet very beautiful. My life seems something like that too – though at times I make it more complicated than it needs to be.*   6.10.2002

One of these complications is an inner beggar I discovered in myself, a part of me that feels it doesn't deserve. Of course, I don't deserve. That's what makes the abundant generosity of the Universe so amazing. It is there, not because we deserve it. It is there because that is how the Divine Mystery has created it. This was brought home to me again and again. Reflecting on a sandplay:

> *I made a figure in the damp sand. She is female and pregnant. She speaks of abundance – full belly, full breasts. She is Earth mother, placid amid all we do on her. Maybe she is also me. She is abundance and I am aware of an abundance in myself. I notice how easily I flow in the role of leading, facilitating and teaching, and at the same time be a fellow traveller with the participants. It is out of the abundance of inner wisdom, grown through opportunities and experiences throughout my life, that my skills and understandings flow. I am astonished whenever I recognise this.*   6.9.2003

Gratitude and abundance are constant themes running through my journals during these years. Even the weather reminds me of abundance:

> *It is raining today. After years of dry conditions, it seems the drought has broken. How welcome is the bounty falling from above, drenching the Earth, racing down rivers, replenishing water storages! Everything looks refreshed and clean. Rain speaks of grace, gratuitously poured on the Earth and on all that lives. Deo Gratias!*   29.10.2003

The pearl on my cross speaks its deep wisdom even more powerfully to me today than it did twenty years ago. And it tells me that this abundance is a shared blessing:

> *All I am and receive is not individually mine. It belongs to All. In the oneness all is shared. Whatever enriches one enriches all; whatever impoverishes one impoverishes all. In my prayer, I embrace the people who come to mind, those suffering in their brokenness, family, people close to me, leaders of governments, and also Saddam Hussein, Osama bin Laden and other people the western world loves to hate. I hold the Pearl that includes the whole human community, the mystical communion in which I also belong. There are no words in this prayer, just wide-awake consciousness, clear as crystal, like the resonance of a bell.*
>   7.8.2004

The pearl reminds me constantly of the value of every experience of my life; each has been a grace – an utterly free and gracious gift of the Unfathomable Mystery we call God, costing not less than everything. Like Mary, I know myself full of grace, and inexpressibly grateful to the One who is the abundant Source of all I am, have and experience. Amazing Grace!

4
The God who disappears

> *A phrase that has been with me this week is 'The God who disappears'. When I was young, God was very present as another Person and in the person of Jesus. Some-where along the journey, the God 'out there' has disappeared. There is no God 'out there'. The 'out there' God has become the inner God; not Someone separated from me, but One who expresses its Self in me, in all creation. Is there a God apart from God's manifestation in every realm of existence? My hunch is that God lives and breathes the Cosmos and the Cosmos lives and breathes God.*   10.4.2004

Of course, I long to experience God as God. I am like Moses who asked to see God's face. God said to him, 'No one can see me and live'. One day, the obvious dawned on me:

> *Of course, I live in darkness in my relationship with God: God is Unknowable Mystery. That's why the Divine Presence seems like absence to me. I don't have the capacity to see God. I am continually drawn into the dark Nothingness of God which is mirrored in my own deep down dark Nothingness. I do not have words for this, but, like an unerring compass, this Dark Mystery draws me on.*

Though Moses couldn't see God, God revealed to him the Divine Name:

> 'The Lord, the Lord, God of tenderness and compassion, slow to anger, rich in faithful love and constancy; for thousands he maintains his kindness, forgives faults, transgression, sin...' (Exodus 34:6).

Can I see the divine qualities of tenderness, kindness, compassion, love, forgiveness and many others in myself, in other people and events? Can I see them in the abundance of creation? in the resilience of life? in the love in the eyes of parents as they gaze at their newborn? That is where God is present among us and within us. Muslims see these qualities as the names of God and have a practice of reciting ninety-nine of them daily. As I contemplate on those 'names' and experience their qualities in my relationships, I find them growing within me. They well up from within, from the God presence within me.

From early in life, I have sought to do God's will. I thought of that as some direction or task in life that God had determined from all eternity. But –

> *What I need to do is to let myself be carried in the current of the Divine Will and Purpose. In some way, I have lived out of a perception that the Divine Will and Purpose and my own will are at odds. At the same time, I have come to see that the Divine Will for me and my part in the Mystery of Being and Becoming is written in the essence of my being. God's will for me is that I BE what I am created to be. I create the struggle to bring my will into harmony with God's. The sufferings and miseries that arise from those struggles are all of my own making. In reality, there is no disharmony.*   19.5.2004

I still had some way to go in learning to trust my inner knowing – my conscience, that 'innermost secret core and sanctuary of a person where I am alone with God whose voice echoes in my depths'.[39] With the passing years this has become more and more real for me: the outer authority needs to be subject to the inner authority, the voice of conscience. When I am living from the centre that is my truth, the Corrie I am created to be, I am like a crystal:

> *The crystal I use for my prayer appeared like a crystal palace, brilliant with light. This is what each of us is called to become. Even our physical bodies are called to become what they truly are: material manifestations of the*

---

39 Cf. Vatican II, *Gaudium et Spes*, art. 16.

> *Spirit. As I write this, I suddenly understand: this is the Transfiguration! Stupendous mystery! Amazing grace!*
> 31.7.2004

On the feast of the Transfiguration:

> *I prayed evening prayer with the awareness of the crystal palace. Called to be luminous with the Divine Presence. We already are that, but my opaqueness hides it. Continue to purify me until I am that luminous crystal palace. And not just on my own, but as belonging in the mystical Body of all humanity, alive and numinous with the life and light of that stupendous Mystery we name God.*
> 6.8.2004

To become the Corrie I am created to be so that the God who disappears can reveal the Divine Self in me and in every created being: that is the core meaning of my life. That is the mystery I am created to live in the ordinary everyday of my life. This is mysticism:

> *Everyday mysticism: that's what comes to me as I let the power of the above realisation permeate my awareness. It isn't about being taken up into the seventh heaven. It is about having my eyes, mind and heart opened to the nature of what is, beyond what appears. It is in the ordinary every day. I simply need to wake up to the astonishing Mystery of the ordinary every day.*
> 1.8.2004

In February 2006, shortly after my father and my older brother died, I did a month-long retreat. The timing was propitious, giving me time and space to grieve and be with the new reality of my life. My mother had died the year before. It felt as though the tectonic plates of my existence had shifted. I had no parental home anymore.

My grief drew me mostly into darkness – the dark mystery of life and death, and the Dark Mystery we call God who drew me deeper and deeper into that Darkness. Father Ken Petersen O.Carm was my spiritual director for that retreat. As I shared with him what was happening in me during those days, he gave me a quote from the Upanishads that spoke profoundly:

> The face of truth remains hidden behind a circle of gold. Unveil it, O God of light, that I who love the true may see!
> O life-giving sun, offspring of the Lord of creation, solitary seer of heaven! Spread thy light and withdraw thy blinding splendour that I may behold thy radiant form: that spirit far away within thee is my own inmost spirit.[40]

It was the hidden face of truth in these verses that caught my attention. For many years, a verse from John's Gospel had been a mantra for me:

> If you make my Word your home, you will indeed be my disciples,
> You will know the truth and the truth will set you free
>
> (John 8:32-34).

It seems I have always yearned to know the Truth. The verses of the Isa Upanishad resonated with that yearning.

The more I pondered the hidden face of Truth, the deeper I was drawn into it. Eventually, I drew a mandala:

> *It's brilliant black with a corona around it – something like the sun in full eclipse.*
>
> *Sitting before it, looking into that black disk that covers the blinding splendour of the Face of God, it seems to move constantly. Brilliant light lights up now one part of the circumference, now another.*
>
> *'You want to see the face of God? Look into me as into a mirror, and you will find me deep within yourself/Self. I am you, as I have told you before.'*

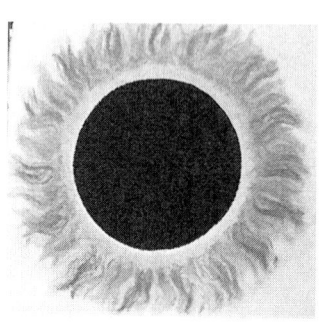

---

40 *Isa Upanishad*, Juan Mascaró translation, *The Upanishads*, Penguin Classics, 1965, p. 49.

Yet, as I looked into the black mirror, even that disappeared. Its brilliant blackness kept shading over with greys and then orange: 'The face of truth remains hidden behind a circle of gold...' The God who disappears!

As I continued to sit with that mandala, I prayed:

> *'Lord, that I may see.'*
> *'You can see. I have given you sight. You just need to forget all you know and BE HERE NOW.'*   22.2.2006

A few days later, I was given to see the black depths of that mandala – and laughed as the joke dawned on me:

> *From the time I first sat with this mandala, there was something about it that reminded me of the Wizard of Oz. I guess that's the joke: What do I anticipate seeing when God's face is unveiled? I, who have always thought of God as Light, didn't ever think of God as Darkness, infinitely deep Darkness. As I sat, laughing at this recognition, I saw myself falling into those dark depths, frolicking in them like a dolphin at play.*
>
> *Physicists tell us that there is no such thing as nothingness, as pure emptiness. What appears to us as such is pure potential. That seems a pertinent image of the Infinite Dark Depths. I look at the black centre of my mandala: any image can arise out of it – my face, the faces of people I know and love. In my mandala, fiery light surrounds the black centre. Paradoxically, light comes from these Dark Depths, colours, forms, power, creation and creativity – everything that is, ever was and is yet to be, comes out of, is a manifestation of, the Dark Face of God. It is so obvious, I might have missed it.*   25.2.2006

Who would have thought that the darkness of grief could lead me into such profound experiences and insights? And there was more to come. It seems to be my experience that grieving happens in some deep region of myself, below my awareness. Every now and then it will come to the surface, usually when something isn't well in my relationship with myself in my current circumstances.

> *I did a session addressing the weariness and anger I have been feeling. I feel resentful for being called upon to meet so many needs and demands and there not being anyone there for me in my needs. Feeling underneath all that, I accessed grief at the loss of home, of Mum and Dad. They were always there, always a home to go back to, knowing I would be welcomed and embraced. I don't have that home anymore. I don't have a family of my own like my brothers and sisters have. I felt again the empty womb and grief for the children I might have had.*
>
> *As I sat within the emptiness of my heart and womb, Elizabeth came to mind – barren until she was past bearing a child. And yet, it could still happen. Then the annunciation: 'May it be...' The words repeated themselves in me. I'm not privy to what 'it' is, but have a sense that something needs to be brought to birth in me. May it be. May it be.*   11.8.2007

Again the sense of being pregnant, of something wanting to come to birth! How frequently it recurs through the years. I never knew what I was to birth. I simply needed to trust that it would reveal itself in the fullness of time. Reflecting on it today, I wonder whether what needed to come to birth within me was the Face of Truth within me, which is my own innermost truth, the Self that is me, yet is infinitely more than my individual being. It is the Self of God in whom all is One.

5
The awesome mission of being human

In 2006, I read *The Passion of the Western Mind* by Rick Tarnas,[41] the fascinating story of western philosophy from the time of the early Greeks to the present. As I came to the final chapter, I reflected:

> *Ideas have consequences. Our thinking and assumptions shape our experiences and vice versa. If it is true that we perceive according to what we bring to our perception, is mental illness brought about by some such dynamic? Is depression an illness in itself? Or is it the result of the way we think, or believe things are or ought to be? Perhaps some utopian dream has driven the human enterprise of science, philosophy, religion, etc. When the results of that endeavour seem ambiguous at best, do we find ourselves adrift in an ocean of uncertainty? Is that where some go into depression or some other psycho-spiritual illness? This poses a challenging question: are we equal to the mission of being human?*   30.12.2006

Am I equal to the mission of being human?

Some days later, a friend said to me, 'What's wrong with you? You're just not yourself.' Her question brought up a wave of emotion within me. As I tuned in to it, I realised that I had become disconnected from myself, preventing me from feeling what was going on within me. I had been on a visit to my family and felt anew the loss of my parents and parental home. On my return, I focused on preparing for the course that was due to begin later that month – an effective way to keep my feelings at bay. My friend's question reminded me to listen to my inner self:

---

41 Richard Tarnas, *The Passion of the Western Mind: Understanding the Ideas that have Shaped our World View*, Penguin Random House, 1991

> *I became aware of the emotional pain I am carrying. I recognise physical pain readily enough, but not emotional pain. I met a deep-seated fear of being in touch with my vulnerability, lest all she carries takes me to breakdown, to not being able to cope. That fear gave rise to my resistance, the fear of helplessness, of not having control over my emotions. From earlier experiences, I know that such breakdown is a great gift of growth and healing, but that isn't enough to ease those fears. Is there a connection here to the uncertainty that both physicists and philosophers come up against – where the ground beneath our feet turns to water? How can I walk with confidence in a condition of fluidity, doubt and fear? I have no control over anything in that condition. But I have choice – to succumb to fear, leading to death, or to surrender in faith and trust, to allow myself to be pulled over the edge of the abyss, into the Infinite Dark Depths of God.* 2.1.2007

I have never seen myself as particularly fearful. But the deep-seated fear of letting go of all my certainties, of *walking out the gate naked*, has challenged me again and again. Like Peter, I am called to walk on water, and, like Peter, I often doubt and sink. If our vocation as human beings is to be mystics, we will meet our fears again and again. And then to remember: I have a choice: to give in to my fears, or to act in faith and trust.

Reflecting on my reading of *The Passion of the Western Mind*;

> *It is a breathtaking account of the trajectory of human understanding of itself, the world and the Cosmos. There are patterns there I also recognise in my own life. Each breakthrough into a new dimension of self-understanding holds an energy of the numinous. It releases me into a larger 'space', giving a sense of breaking through to freedom. As we grow into that space and fill it with our enlarged sense of self, it loses its energy and starts to constrict us. Then we search for openings that will release us from the womb that no longer serves as a growing space.*

We go through a dying phase before we come to a rebirth in a new dimension.

In our time, it seems that we have dismantled all the traditional certainties and pushed them to the limit. We find ourselves in the death throes of expulsion from those certainties and the world they created. But those death throes may also be a birth process. The world we are being born into will be a reclaiming of the feminine, a re-membering in the primal oneness of all being. This is a breathtaking way of understanding the times we live in.
8.1.2007

'A reclaiming of the feminine.' The theme of the feminine continued to arise during these years, usually drawing my attention to itself through my body.

I was feeling tired and unwell, not physically unwell, but more like a sickness of soul. I knew I needed to work with those feelings, but I felt strong resistance to doing so:

Resistance, denial, fear – not a fear I can feel. It is deeper than that – residing in the bowels of the earth, powerfully exerting its 'no'. A fear, a terror at the level of existence itself, binding me hand and foot, controlling my spirit with an iron hand. It feels ancient, so much part of my life that I haven't seen it.

When I meet such resistance, I really need to address the issue that gave rise to it. I organised a session for myself:

I met the controller in me. He is a heavyweight, rigid, inflexible. There is no give in him. He sees it as his job to keep the world in order, running smoothly. I saw how this energy has forged my identity: reliable, dependable, thorough. If I step out of his controlling energy, if I lose control, I lose myself, the self I know myself to be, the self others know me to be. I suspect that is what the terror is about. And its consequence?

> *In the session I also met a mad woman. She went mad because 'they' controlled her, took her power and her voice. In the end, the only way out for her was to go mad, to go completely out of control mad. She spoke, she sobbed and raved in her madness and despair. I felt no emotional connection with her, but her madness and terror expressed itself in me with great intensity.* 15.7.2007

I asked myself: Is this woman part of me? Or is she an archetype whose energy is in me? I was terrified of her madness. If I stepped out of the power of the controller, would I find myself mad like her? Some deep trust was called for here, trust to face my fear and befriend this mad woman.

In the following days and weeks, I began to get some insights: my heavyweight controller is a head character, very rational and logical. The mad woman is not rational. She is a gut character and represents my instinctual energies. When I spoke about her in spiritual direction, Ken suggested that she holds creative energy. If so, and I set her free, she could contribute her gifts. Her wild energy does not need to send me mad. It can spice my life!

As the months passed, this feminine presence continued to arise. There was a dimension in her that was personal to me. But another encounter suggested that she also held the collective frustrations of women in a patriarchal world:

> *A tightness in my shoulder felt like a heavy hand, a strong grip, holding me tightly. As I 'listened' to it, I met a woman who had been banished from her village community since childhood and wandered in dark and desolate regions, lost and unkempt. Her name – which she didn't know until it was told her during this session – was Alisha. When we looked up its meaning, we found it was 'one protected by God, noble and kind'!* 17.10.2007

And there was another woman – perhaps she is Woman, the collective. She railed and railed against the Church in which she had been locked up, made a Christian though that wasn't what she knew herself to be; made her forget her innate wisdom and ancient healing ways; older than Jesus, a follower of Jesus, and full of anger at the Church for purporting to speak his message in his name while it doesn't really know Jesus and understand who he is and what he stands for. She stayed locked in because of the fear of the devil getting her if she stepped out – a fear the Church instilled into her. 18.10.2007

I was surprised at her vehemence. Like many women I know, I experience my share of frustration at the institutional Church with its patriarchal authority. But to meet the depth and power of this woman's rage was confronting: Do I have the courage to let it in and own it as our collective experience as women?

In a session towards the end of that year, I met yet another a woman. Earlier that year, there had been an issue with a woman to whom we had offered hospitality. The issue had been resolved, but what happened with this woman continued to bother me. I needed to find what it was in me that seemed somehow stuck to her. That's how I met the next woman:

What came to me was a shadow of a woman, lost, insubstantial, wandering the desert places, shut out from human companionship, stuck in darkness. She wanted to find her body, her substance, and come into the light. The darkness clung to her like glue. 'Out of darkness into light': my therapist repeated this as a mantra, calling her forth. It seemed to vibrate over a great distance, creating a bridge that reached in and drew her into the light. Uncertain at first, like a newborn adjusting to its new reality, she experienced herself as woman. She needed a name. We invited her to listen for her name. After a few moments she heard it: Beloved! As she spoke it, the Light flowed through her, 'I am Beloved of the Beloved! I am light, light from Light, Beloved of the Beloved'. 19.12.2007

I don't know the connection between The Beloved and the woman who had been bothering me. The realms of the collective unconscious are mysterious. My sense was that the Beloved belonged to some other time. Having been instrumental in setting her free, I was freed from the woman my psyche couldn't let go.

The Beloved of the Beloved is what woman is. Hers is a power, beauty and grace which she desires to contribute to the Church and to the world at large. She can only do so when these are open to receive them, when they surrender their patriarchal control, not only over women, but also over the Earth. Perhaps the title of this chapter should be: *The awesome mission of being Woman*, the mission of contributing to the world from the fullness of womanhood.

However, patriarchy is not to be equated with men or maleness, even if in practice it favours men. Patriarchy is an archetypal energy, as are the masculine and the feminine. The women I met in my inner exploration are manifestations of the feminine archetype. They were part of me insofar as I had absorbed their energy, but they were more than me. The patriarchal masculine that I had also absorbed is destructively controlling, as is evident in the sessions described above. A healthy masculine brings strong qualities such as truth, justice, integrity, virtues our world desperately needs.

Father Bede Griffiths, the British Benedictine monk, moved from Britain to India to find 'the other half of his soul', the feminine dimension of his psyche. That's what the patriarchal world also needs to do: to find the other half of its soul, to let go of the patriarchal system that rules by control, domination and suppression, that favours the strong and uses the weak to its own purposes. It isn't about rejecting the masculine. Rather, what is needed, as Bede Griffiths says, is a marriage of the predominantly masculine West to the predominantly feminine East. This can bring a very different energy to governance and leadership and ways of being in the world – exercising authority as *power with*, rather than *power over*; listening and responding rather than imposing preconceived ideas or desires. That way of governing constantly keeps the good of the whole in mind in its decision making. It values and incorporates qualities of both the masculine and the feminine, in us as individuals and as society, for all of us have access to the qualities of both.

While pondering these things, a memory from my long retreat comes back. At the time, I was conscious of my deep longing to know the Oneness of God; yet I knew only separateness:

Perhaps our fundamental sin is separateness, not knowing who we truly are. I look at the crucifix: This is my body broken for you. I 'see' an image of him split down the middle, the two halves parted like a curtain and revealing the awful depths of Darkness. I became aware of the horrifying things we human beings do to one another: oppression, slavery, torture, holocausts and killing fields, starvation, war... In desiring to know the Oneness, do I really want to know and own as my own, humankind's totality? Oneness in sanctity, yes; but oneness in sin on an horrific scale? I recoil from the horror of it. Here is a mystery beyond my understanding. I would prefer a golden circle over that chasm, and live as though it isn't there. And yet... remove the veil that I may see my true Face and know it is yours, and the true face of every person, every creature. 27.2.2006

The image of the crucified Jesus cleft in two visited me several more times over the following years, each time showing the horrors of human sin in the cleft of his broken body. Why is it coming back to me at this stage? Could this image of Jesus' broken body, the halves parted by the horrors of human sin, be pointing to our world's need to embrace its suppressed feminine? As I ponder that question, it dawns on me: When a people or society identifies itself with the masculine half of its soul and suppresses the feminine half, we disconnect from the fullness of our humanity. Power, greed and ambition take over, resulting, not only in the suppression of women, but in all the social ills that cause the suffering of our world, setting people and nations violently against each other, raping the Earth to the extent that its ability to sustain life is now critically endangered.

The rent body of the crucified Christ is a symbol of what humanity does to itself when it lives from only the masculine half of its soul, causing all the horrors we humans visit on one another. The awesome mission of being human demands that we, individually and collectively, mend that split by finding and integrating the feminine half of our soul and fostering the virtues of the healthy masculine. Only then can the healing that people, communities, and the world so desperately need come about.

6
The BEholder

The volume of work on my desk had piled up. Stressing to get on top of it, I became inundated by it. I was beyond stepping back far enough to prioritise the urgent matters and decide which could wait. Even when not at my desk, my mind was preoccupied with all I 'had' to do. It was a familiar pattern.

At some moment I stopped and took a deep breath. I became aware of what was happening within myself. Stressing to catch up with all I 'had' to do, had lost touch with my still centre, my Self. I remembered something I had read about Shakti and Shiva, gods in the Hindu tradition:

> *Shakti is the universal principle of energy, power and creativity, always moving, at play through the cycles of creation, destruction and recreation. Shiva is the beholder of Shakti, the still point that holds her dynamism. Without Shiva, all would be chaos. Without Shakti, there would be nothing but static inertia. These two principles, one masculine, the other feminine, are eternally in creative dance. The Cosmos is the fruit of their dance. Within every dynamic creation there is a static force, a still centre, the still point of the whirling Universe, and of the inner Universe that is me.* 10.6.2006

It struck me that, in my busyness, my Shakti energy had taken over and I had lost touch with my inner Shiva, the Beholder. To behold is more than giving something a cursory glance. It is to take in what one sees, to *hold the BEing* of what one contemplates. When I lose myself in my Shakti energy, I am no longer holding my BEing.

Pondering on this, I reflect on the Trinity:

> *Contemplating the Mystery of the Trinity from the Still Point of the BE-holder, I see myself as the Cosmic creation, as the expression of the dance of the Trinity – the Father as the still point, the BE-holder, the Spirit as*

> *the restless energy, creative power, ever at play enlivening the Incarnate Universe, the Word made flesh in and as creation. This is profound Mystery. It is dynamically present in me, in us, in every nook and cranny of the Cosmos. I am the BE-holder; I am the creative Spirit; I am the fruit of both, the Word made flesh, embodying the Divine Mystery.*   11.6.2006

The recognition that creation comes to into *BEing* within the very life of the Trinity is truly astonishing. It means that creation shares in the very nature of the Trinitarian life, born from the dynamic relationship within the Trinity. That being so, then relationship is of the essence of the Cosmos and of our being within the Cosmos. Every being can only BE in relationship with every other being. Modern physics has also discovered this.

Continuing to ponder the pattern of relationship within the Trinity, I begin to see it also as the pattern of my Being:

> *In my prayer, I continue to come home to the Still Point. There 'the jar of meal is not spent and the oil never runs out' (1 Kings 17:16). There the burden of insufficiency drops away. There is always enough for the task at hand and for my BEing. The Divine BE-holder does just that: holds my BEing in all fulness. I, in my ego fears and anxieties, create insufficiency. Yet the Infinite Divine Source is expressing Itself in me.*   13.6.2006

'To be Christian is to be contemplative', said Ken, when I shared these insights in my spiritual direction session. I think we can equally say, to be human is to be contemplative. For it is in contemplation, in coming into the Still Point of the BEholder, that we truly find ourselves in conscious communion with ourselves, and beyond ourselves, with the Mystery of the Trinity creatively present in every BEing. There all our activity finds creative order and fruitfulness, no matter what chaos storms on the surface.

Twelve months later, the Mystery of the Trinity further reveals its immediacy in my life. It came from a realisation that we become who we are as we express who we are in our lives:

> *We become who we are by enacting our self. Enacting what we are not makes us what we are not. I am, you are, the Cosmos is, the Divine embodied, the Self-Expression of the Ultimate Mystery we call God. All creation on every plane of Being is the Divine Self-Enactment. Yet I enact what I am not. And to become what I am I need to become what I am not: to enact/live Nothingness. I am seeing it this morning with a clarity and directness that takes my breath away.*
>
> *I am looking at my woven icon: shadows mysteriously revealing a face, and beyond the face, a depth of serene stillness, a silent presence that always moves me.*   5.6.2007

As years have passed, the Mystery of the Trinity has become more and more real for me. Today's theologians have drawn on the insights of modern science and cosmology to give further insights the mystery of God as Trinity. The dynamic of Trinitarian life is also the dynamic of the self-creating Cosmos. In contemplation, the immediacy of the Mystery catches my being up in Itself. The experience is full of paradox:

> *I am aware of the deeper Mystery within and beyond all that exists. I know this Mystery even while I am in a state of not knowing. I've lost the personal and interpersonal in my relationship with the Unknowable One, and yet it is more profoundly personal. It isn't so much 'Be imitators of Christ' as 'For me, to live is Christ'. I am to become what I am, i.e. the Christ. It is about surrendering myself into the Self, my separate individuality into the Oneness of the One. I relate, not to an 'out there' God, but as one enfolded in, permeated by that Ultimate Mystery we call*

God. 'The Father and I are one', as Jesus says in John 10:30.
24.6.2007

While at times I seem to be far from the Still Point within me, I notice a growing awareness of the BEholder. One afternoon, during a breath session in a Grof training workshop, things became rather chaotic in the room. I was supporting a participant from a place of inner stillness, the place of the BEholder. Observing how intensely the other three facilitators were working with people, I asked myself: what do I bring to this work? The response that welled up from within was 'Dadirri', the contemplative stillness that Aboriginal Wisdom Woman, Miriam Rose Ungunmerr-Baumann, speaks about:

> To know me is to breathe with me. To breathe with me is to listen deeply. To listen deeply is to connect. There is a sound, deep calling to deep: Dadirri, the deep inner spring inside us. It calls on us and we call on it.[42]

In that chaotic scene, I was 'the still point of the turning world', holding the place of the BEholder from which order could return.

Traditionally, the Blessed Trinity has been named Father, Son and Holy Spirit. But it seems to me that the Trinity is equally a very feminine symbol. The BEholder is the pregnant One who births from her depths One who is her full self-expression, the Son, whom we also know as Sophia, Lady Wisdom. She, in the dynamism of the life-giving Spirit, gives birth to the self-creating Universe ever in process of BEcoming. If there is truth in what I wrote above, that we become what we are by enacting ourselves, perhaps God is also becoming what God is as she expresses herself in creation.

Of course, God is neither male nor female. Yet both are strongly symbolic of God's way of creating and being with creation. Both the masculine and the feminine are embedded in the Cosmos, the dynamic living image of the Divine.

---

42 Miriam Rose Ungunmerr-Bauman, *Dadirri*, op.cit. I first learnt about Dadirri many years earlier, in an article by Miriam Rose. I have often returned to her simple formula of Dadirri, from which we connect from the heart with one another and with our natural environment.

As I reflect on the unfolding Mystery of the Trinity in the context of my life, I see that the seed of these insights was sown in me many years earlier, during that retreat at John Fisher College in Tasmania, when I heard, 'The Word was made flesh and her name is Corrie'. That experience set me on the journey of probing the mystery of the Incarnation. As I grew into a living incarnational spirituality, I was led into the Mystery of the Trinity. Perhaps that shouldn't surprise me: historically, it was the mystery of Christ that led the early Church into the Mystery of the Trinity.

In 2011 Agnes Ryan mss died. I had known her since I was in my teens, and in her later years we became close friends. A few days after her death, during my morning meditation, a question dropped into my mind:

> *Agnes, who are you now? Are you still Agnes? Or are you that part of God that has had the experience of being Agnes?*

The question startled me. I had not been thinking of her when it came to me so unexpectedly. But I have pondered it frequently since. If, as I believe, the entire created Cosmos is the Word of God incarnate, then perhaps it is also true to say that I am a tiny fragment of God having the experience of being Corrie in every breath I take. Wow! And if this is true of Agnes and of me, it is true of every created being. God cannot be fragmented. It is God who is having the experience of being Corrie, of being that pigeon, of being the Milky Way. Wow!

Such insights into the Mystery of God are not given so that I might withdraw from the challenges and chaos of our world. Rather, I am to be drawn more deeply into them. God BEholds with the eye of Love, drawing what God BEholds into a relationship of love. As I am drawn ever more deeply into that relationship, my BEholding takes on the qualities of the Divine BEholding. I am drawn into a relationship of love with the one I am BEholding. Here mysticism becomes prophetic:

> *The only thing that will save us from destroying the Earth and ourselves is mysticism. The government is*

planning to drain wetlands to conserve water. But the more we interfere with Earth's ecological systems, the more problems we create. Then we interfere still more to address those problems. We need a new vision, new eyes to see the whole, eyes informed by the consciousness of mystics who see the oneness and interrelatedness of all that exists, and our human species as one tiny fibre in that oneness. We still seem to think we own it all by divine right.   23.4.2007

In my younger years, I thought mysticism was for rare individuals who were drawn into the heights of the Divine, leaving the rest of us ordinary folk in the struggles of life here below. Now I know that mysticism is for everyone, no matter who we are, no matter what religion or culture we are born into. When we are present from within, from our inner BEholder, we become aware of a mysterious depth in the ordinary every day, the presence of the Sacred in every being. The mystic is one who sees with the eye of heart, the eye of love. In that seeing, the ordinary and the familiar are revealed as extraordinary:

Ordinariness! When something is familiar to us, it is ordinary – even while it is extraordinary. And that is beautiful. When things are as they are, when life is what it is, we are in the ordinary – at home here. Without the at-homeness, I can't appreciate the ordinary for what it is. I will seek the extraordinary out there. And I will never find it, for at-homeness can only be found in appreciating the now-moment in all its extraordinary ordinariness – amazingly wondrous.   11.10.2007

All these ponderings bring me back to the question, who am I? I am blessed with these profound insights, but who am I really?

The older I get, the harder it is to know how to answer. Each of us is unfathomable mystery, a unique expression of the Mystery of God. I can give my name and describe observable details about myself, but I am not that. There is a knowing that isn't expressible in words, concepts or images. These merely hint at what is beyond them. That I am at all is a matter of profound wonder. I need not have been, yet here I am. And I am part of a family, a community, a web of life and existence as immediate as the space my body occupies and infinite in its cosmic dimensions. 25.1.2009

I can only respond with profound gratitude in and to the One who is Trinity.

7
Lay your eggs and move on

From time to time during 2007, I experienced a restlessness in myself. Sometimes it came in a sense of 'I want out'. It might arise when I felt pressured by the amount of work to be done, when I was facing a task that took me beyond my comfort zone, or when I was feeling blocked about the way forward. The reaction was always 'I want out'. I wrote:

> *It struck me this morning that this sense of 'I want out' is manifestation of a pattern that may well go back to the pattern of my birth.1 As I reflect on this, I remember my feeling of dark despair in our early years in Tulendeena when it seemed we would never get out of the black hole of poverty. But we did move out of it, and I moved out of that despair. Yet something of the fear and anxiety of it can still raise their spectre in the background.* 2.4.2007

> *My longing to 'get out' may also be fuelled by the lure of the Infinite. 'You have seduced me, Lord, and I have allowed myself to be seduced' (Jeremiah 20:7). Living at the intersection of my earthly humanity and the call to transcendence into Ultimate Mystery, holding both within myself – perhaps that is the most fundamental level of this pain.* 3.4.2007

A few days later, on Good Friday:

> *Something has shifted in me. The sense of urgency, 'I want out', has left me, as has the pressure of preparation for the next course module. The work remains, but I am not burdened by its pressure. I am in a quiet space, a 'nowhere' space. I feel as though I have stepped into another reality, like stepping into an inner chamber where the noise and pace of this everyday-world fade into the distance. I become still, alert, simply present, no words, no thoughts, no desires, no sense of pain or elation. It is*

like death, except I am aware, aware of the state I am experiencing. And it is good to be here.   6.4.2007

The inner stillness remained with me the following days:

I awoke early this morning and sat at the open window: a slender crescent moon lit the river in silver in the dark Earth. All was at peace. Somewhere a kookaburra laughed to waken the dawn. Ever so gradually, the eastern sky began to lighten, creating soft rosy tints on the far cloud banks. The new creation is emerging out of the night's darkness. I felt a mirroring of it all in my soul. The weariness and emotional fragility that has weighed on me of late has given way to a quiet peace that, like this brand-new morning, is ready to take up the life of this new day.   15.4.2007

These observations come from my BEholder. In that place, my inner stillness is like a mirror that takes in and reflects the outer world in all its sacredness. I also notice that, when I am fully present in the moment, I see the depth dimension of my surroundings. It is as though I perceive, not only the beings that fill the space around me, but the space itself, connecting me to all I see and connecting those beings with each other. That space seems to embrace us in one sacred relationship permeating us all.

While my restlessness had gone, something still suggested that the time was coming to move on. On to what? I was tired and I knew I needed to take a break after the completion of our training course. But there seemed to be something else:

In a guided reflection this afternoon, I was looking at a river, inviting it to speak. What came to my ears was, 'move on, move on, move on'. It is a sense that I am leaving this work.   17.6.2007

The sense of leaving the work that I loved and found so rewarding came as something of a surprise. Moving on is the nature of our missionary lives. Our motto is 'Go into the highways and byways'. Literally and metaphorically, mobility was part of our spirit and of our lived reality. Still, sometimes I would have liked to stay put, to see come to fruition what I had been instrumental in nurturing.

I had received an earlier hint that the time was coming to move on. At a group workshop in Toowoomba in October 2006, we were invited to draw a card from a pack and listen to its message. The card I drew was of a beautiful Ulysses butterfly. It spoke to me of grace, emergence, transformation, perfection, gentleness, and also of fickleness. Its message to me was, 'Lay your eggs of life and move on'.

At some stage during 2007, I mentioned to Bernadette, our leader at the time, that I wanted to take three months long service leave at the end of the year. I also mentioned that I had a sense that, sometime in the future, I needed to write, though I did not know what I needed to write about. Bernadette encouraged me not only to take the break, but to follow up the sense that I needed to write and to do this the next year, rather than leave it to some indefinite future time. I took a gulp: That would mean closing down the premises that had served as my workplace. I knew that, given my age, I probably would not return to full-time practice. Was I ready for this? As I listened for wisdom from my heart, I heard, 'You've laid your eggs, so move on'.

The year was drawing to an end. We were in the final module of our training course. Its theme was separation, death and rebirth. It focused on letting go the losses of the past, and also those the group was facing as the training course came to an end and they would disperse. They had journeyed deeply with one another. Saying goodbye to that would not be easy. At the same time, it was important that they were aware of what they had gained. We asked them to invite an image to speak to them of the fruits of their work this year.

Knowing I was moving on yet again, I invited an image that could speak of the fruits of my life. I saw in my mind's eye a winding road with little white daisies growing on the verges:

> *It is a beautiful image of my life: no footprints or monuments, but little white daisies bringing beauty and joy to those who have eyes to see. And that's what the vision did to my heart. I am deeply grateful. Footprints and monuments eventually erode away. The daisies, which*

last only a few hours, will continue to seed and bloom, generation after generation. 14.11.2007

The message is the same as that of the Ulysses butterfly. I may never see the fruits of what I have sown during my life. Travellers on the road of my image will not know who sowed those daisies. I am called to trust that, in God's good time, the work will bear fruit. I have sown my seed and, as Paul reminds us, someone else will water it and do the harvesting, but it is all God's work (cf. 1 Corinthians 3:6).

Some years later, aware of the enormous suffering and dysfunction in our world, I questioned myself:

What have I done in my seventy years that has made a difference? It seems to me to be very little. Then I reflect on what we know of Jesus' life.
He didn't take on the world's big issues in the world's big way. He simply lived out his awareness of his relationship with his Father in all around him. He touched those he met. For some, that touch was transformative in one way, for others it had the opposite effect, depending on how they perceived and responded to him. Yet so profound was his simple presence that its ripples continue to our times. His Spirit continues to wash over us, transforming all according to the way they perceive and respond. Some respond in amazing works. Others in unspectacular ways. What matters is the willingness to respond as she breathes on us and in us. 27.6.2011

Perhaps there are times when my touch, too, is transformative:

Yesterday I met a woman whose whole being seemed wracked with pain. As I spoke to her, she started to cry.

> *I held her as she cried and cried out to God for help. I spoke to her about Tolle's pain-body and asked her could she see it. At first, she could not, but after a while she could. It was her heart. I suggested she hold her heart tenderly, with kindness and love. When she said she was holding her heart, I told her God was holding her heart with her hands. We sat quietly, she still weeping. After a while she said, 'I went somewhere. I don't know where, but something happened'. I felt very moved by the whole event that happened so spontaneously. The Mystery permeates everything.* 17.11.2011

It is all God's work, touching people as we touch them. A couple of weeks later, another chance encounter turned out to be a sacred moment:

> *'May I ask you something? Are you happy?' This question was put to me at the wedding celebration last night. I don't remember ever being asked that question in the way John asked it. It came from his soul-search and deep desire for which he found no space in the world of his everyday environment – a sense of despair, yet a hope beyond despair, however dimly glimpsed. As we conversed, I knew I was on sacred ground, the place where pain and joy meet.* 12.12.2011

Brief encounters, then each of us goes our own way. Yet each encounter touches something deep within each of us. A seed sown? An egg laid? Noel Connolly ssc calls such encounters *organic mission*. They happen in unexpected moments and arise out of the quality of presence we bring to our encounters.

Part VII

Dying to Live

1
Living in an evolving universe

Hidden beyond our grasp, in the depth of the future that forever takes us and our world into itself, there resides the really real... Evolution demands that we think of God as drawing the world from up ahead, attracting it forward into the future.[43]

As I come to the final decade of my journal journey, I am aware that I have many more years behind me than ahead of me. This is not a morbid awareness. Rather, I experience a growing appreciation of the gift of life, given moment by moment. It is a precious grace, calling me to live into it as fully and creatively as I may. The quote from John Haught (above) speaks to me about this. God is drawing me and all creation *from up ahead*, into a future that only becomes visible as we live into it.

It is over twenty-five years since I read the *Tao of Physics* and woke up to the Universe as being vastly more wondrous than most of us are aware of in our day-to-day lives. It is in a continual process of evolution, the unfolding of its inner potential to become more than it is. The Cosmos is like one great organism which has unfolded in myriad, unique expressions, each of which, while a whole in itself, remains part of the greater whole. When I caught a glimpse of this reality, I was blown away by it. The perspective it opens up challenges our understanding of everything, even of God.

During a community retreat, we watched Brian Swimme's DVD, *The Journey of the Universe*. One of the questions we were invited to reflect on was: How did it all start, this awesome quest?

This awesome quest? What is this awesome quest?

- *Is it that first flaring forth that started the birthing of the Universe?*
- *Is it the quest of the Universe?*

---

43 John Haught, *Mystery and Promise: A Theology of Revelation*, Liturgical Press, 1993.

- *Is it God's quest, unfolding in the Universe?*
- *Is all the questing, including that of my life and of the life of MSS, really a participation in the Divine Quest?*
- *And could it be that this entire creative endeavour is God seeking what God is/can become?*

These questions take me into a great silence of awe and wonder, of Presence and Mystery.   24.3.2014

This awesome quest! When I was young, I saw this quest as about me-and-God. My journals show how, through the years, my understanding has been stretched until now it incorporates the whole of reality. I am no longer the centre of the Universe. I am one being among countless other beings. This perspective also shapes our mission:

Sitting in the awareness of this journey, what comes to me is that my mission is God. Reflecting further on that mission, I see that the ordinary every day, the particular expression of the Gospel that is MSS, the growing awareness and appreciation of creation and so on, are integrally part of that core mission. Essentially, it is being-in-relationship, open to the dynamic flow of life that is one great act of death giving birth which is God's birth in creation. The Divine shimmers in and through the entire Cosmos as Love, Presence, as its Life Force, its profound tenderness and its fierce destructive forces, including human hatred, violence, oppression and injustice. These latter are difficult to incorporate into my understanding. Our mission, the Gospel imperative, is to transform them into justice, love, peace through mercy and forgiveness.   28.8.2014

How do we fulfil this Gospel imperative in practice? Australia was a year into its Royal Commission into Institutional Responses to Child Abuse:

> *I continue to be shocked at the extent of the abuse, and I grieve – I grieve for all who have been abused, the children first of all. Their suffering continues throughout life, and is aggravated by the refusal of those in authority to meet them pastorally. Instead, the victims meet with the cold hard world of legalism... And I grieve for the Church, so badly betrayed by its shepherds, including authorities in Rome who reinstated a priest who had been suspended by his bishop for his abuse of children.* 13.8.2014

How do we address such grievous wrong in a way that brings healing to the suffering victims as well as to their perpetrators? And how do we address the grievous wrong of our Church leadership, failing to act when abuse came to their attention, or, instead of receiving the victims with compassion, turning to the law to protect the reputation of the Church? Where do we find the Divine shimmering in this mess? How might the Divine Spirit weave such devastating wrongs into the evolutionary process of the Cosmos?

In 2014, Jill McCorquodale, my spiritual director, told me about Cynthia Bourgeault's book, *The Holy Trinity and the Law of Three*. I bought a copy and read it right through to get an overview:

> *I have completed my first reading of* The Holy Trinity and the Law of Three. *In it, Cynthia paints a vast, dynamic, hopeful visionary image of the Mystery of God as Trinity, of cosmogenesis and the journey ahead of us. While I have only grasped the barest outline of her vision, I feel energised and excited by it. It taps into that hunger for God that has been with me all my life. For that vision to become organically part of me – or I of It – is sheer grace, beyond my power to realise. I can study, reflect and pray... then wait in joyful hope.* 26.8.2014

In this book, Cynthia shows how an understanding of the law of three can take us beyond dualism into the creative process of what she calls a ternary dynamic. The opposites of dualism cannot move beyond their status quo. But a ternary dynamic brings in a third factor which can hold the opposites in a larger perspective, out of which can arise a new possibility. She writes:

> One can only imagine how greatly the political and religious culture wars could be eased by this simple courtesy of the Law of Three:
>
> 1. the enemy is not the problem but the opportunity;
> 2. the problem will never be solved through eliminating or silencing the opposition but only through creating a new field of possibility large enough to hold the tension of the opposites and launch them in a new direction.
>
> Imagine what a different world it would be if these two precepts were internalised and enacted.[44]

Reflecting on the Law of Three, I wonder, could it help us find a way beyond the good and evil divide? In 2015, Pope Francis called for a Holy Year of Mercy. Mercy could well be the third factor that enables a breakthrough in situations of intractable conflict such as the Israel-Palestinian situation and many others in our world.

A further question arises in me as I reflect on the dynamic of the Law of Three and our struggle to understand evil: Could it be that evil is somehow a necessary ingredient in the creative process? Might it be the irritant that forces us to creative solutions? In *Revelations of Divine Love*, Julian of Norwich writes, 'Sin is necessary, but all will be well'. She doesn't explain the necessity and I haven't come to a way of thinking through such questions, but from my limited understanding of evolution, it seems that the new develops particularly when conditions put significant stress on living beings so that they either evolve or become extinct. Coming to think of it: isn't this 'necessity' also evident in my own life? My journals so clearly show that it is precisely in my failures and brokenness that the new develops.

---

44 Cynthia Bourgeault, *The Holy Trinity and the Law of Three*, Mahwah, NJ, Paulist Press, 1978, pp. 39-40.

The more I attend to my experience of creation, the more I become aware of the Mystery at the heart of it all. The immediacy of that experience has been greatly enriched by my reading about the discoveries of science regarding our evolutionary Universe and also by the theology coming from the dialogue between science and faith. At times I feel dizzy at the vistas these open up for me. The little world of my youth has become the vast Cosmos, and I am part of it. Its 13.8-billion-year history is my history. Often I am lost for words to express the effect this realisation has on me.

Returning from a few days in the mountains with our walking club, I wrote:

> *The grandeur of those vistas of mountains and escarpments dropping down hundreds of metres into deep valleys below was breathtaking and awesome. We camped on top of an escarpment, looking out on such magnificence. At night we watched the light change and soften as the sun sank towards the horizon; we watched the mist rise from the valley far below. As it filled that valley, we saw it light up brilliantly by the light of the full moon.*
>
> *On Sunday night, we sat on rocks still warm from the day's sunlight and reflected together on what draws us to these places, to take in our stride the pain of tired muscles, of breathlessness as we walk up steep mountain tracks. The experience takes us into another way of being, of deep connection with ourselves, with one another and with the Earth in this place. There is profound simplicity and companionship in sharing such experiences. The beauty of the rugged wilderness evokes my sense of wonder and awe, appreciation and gratitude, the privilege of being there, of having the health and strength and wherewithal to visit such places.* 27.1.2016

For me, such experiences are Eucharist, food for body, soul and spirit. They nurture our communion with one another and with All there is. Here the liturgical celebration becomes cosmic, embracing the totality of the Divine Mystery incarnate in creation, the Spirit enlivening the whole and every individual part of that totality. Such communion includes communion in the suffering involved in the evolutionary process of the Cosmos and of its every being, a realisation that has been growing in me over a number of years. During my retreat in 2011, I expressed it in a poem, *Cosmic Eucharist*, included at the end of this chapter.

My consciousness of that communion has continued to deepen through the years. Creation is no longer something outside myself, I am essentially part of it, a tiny organ in the functioning of the whole. One day, sitting on the bank of the upper Yarra River at Warburton, observing the interrelationship and interdependence of all the living and non-living beings that make up that river in that place, I asked myself: What is the ecosystem in which I belong? Until that moment, I had never adverted to my being part of an ecosystem. But what is it that enables me to be, that sustains my life, growth and development?

I began to name the elements of that ecosystem, identifying layer upon layer of beings, each dependent on the next layer and stretching wider and wider in space and time until it encompassed the entire Cosmos, reaching back to its very beginning and to the Divine Source of all that is, the Source that is at once its creative dynamism and its lifeblood. As I caught a vision of its entirety, it took my breath away. Words cannot adequately contain that multidimensional reality. I lapse into awed silence.

And the cosmic 'we' are still in the process of becoming. Brian Swimme says that it takes a Universe this big for us to be here:

> I look at a photo of new-born Olivia, my great niece, and see her as fourteen billion years in the making! How wondrous is that! Everything that exists in the Cosmos has its source, its origin in the creative process set in motion in the Big Bang, when God said, 'Let there BE...' (Genesis 1). The process continues. I am only the briefest moment in the Cosmic becoming. I receive what has come to be at this stage of history, play my brief part and surrender all I am for the next generation of becoming. And not just me, but together and united with every creature that is – in the flow of receiving and surrendering. Whether we are aware of it or not, even if we resist it, we are in its flow.
> 10.2.2021

All creation is continually drawn to become more than what it is, drawn into its potential. I discovered that this insight is actually 'hidden' in the Our Father. One day, on the spur of the moment, I looked up Matthew's version (Matthew 6:9-13) in the Greek interlinear Bible. I noticed in the Greek, the phrase, *Thy will be done*, does not include *done*. The literal translation given is *let-be-being-becoming the will of you*. That suggests to me that God's will is not primarily something we must *do*. Rather, God's desire for creation is that we *be* and that in *being* we continually *become* all that we potentially are. This Divine Desire is at the heart of our *be*ing. The unique gift we human *be*ings bring is conscious awareness of our *becoming* within and as the community of creation.

Evolution happens in relationship and interrelationship; every being dependent on other beings while also nourishing and sustaining other beings in our ecosystem; ecosystems mutually nourishing and sustaining one another; planets, solar systems and galaxies in dynamic relationship with one another, all in the flow of mutual giving and receiving, that creation may continue to unfold into its potential as it journeys into its future.

I belong in this world of inter-being. I know the shrubs and plants in my garden individually. Many of them I have watched grow from slips given to me by friends or strangers. They continue to connect me with the people and places they come from. I grieve when a storm snaps the young tree I planted and nurtured since it was little more than a seedling, watching it grow tall and strong. Its vitality and beauty have given me so much joy. And now I find it on the ground, broken off at its root in a storm. I cannot just throw it away. I dispose of it in a ritual which I perform with appreciation, grateful for all it has brought into my life.

Reverently, I cut off its branches and break up its trunk before placing it in the compost bin. As it breaks down, it will provide food for other plants and trees. And then – surprise, surprise: I find two healthy shoots coming up from its butt. They will grow into a new tree, drawing life from the nutrients stored in the roots of its young parent. Wondrously, life continues!

When I go for my early morning walks, I try to do so consciously. When I walk with all my senses open and receptive, I am alive to my surroundings. I welcome the gently dawning day, greet the trees and shrubs, birds, people and animals I meet along my way. Like familiar friends, they nourish me, body, soul and spirit.

Of course, I do not always walk so consciously present to my surroundings. Often I am like the poet, Rabindranath Tagore:

> On the day when the lotus bloomed, alas,
> my mind was straying, and I knew it not.
> My basket was empty, and the flower remained unheeded...[45]

Is our 'absence' of real presence also what makes us humans such a destructive species on this Earth? We have lost sight of our dependence on our ecosystem and our responsibility to care for it and nourish it while it also cares for and nourishes us. Far too slowly are we waking up to the realisation that, if we continue in the direction we have taken over recent history, we will destroy 'the hand that feeds us'. Again and again, we are warned that we are pushing to the brink Earth's capacity to nurture and sustain life, and yet..!

While countless people have woken up to the urgency of the ecological condition of the Earth, until now too many vested interests hold the power to prevent the fundamental changes needed to pull us back from the brink. They talk 'green' but when it comes to acting on behalf of the Earth, they nibble at the edges while supporting industries that pollute land, atmosphere and waters, destroy ecosystems and habitats, cause the extinction of species in alarming numbers, hasten global warming which in turn causes extreme weather events resulting in natural disaster after natural disaster, impacting most on the lives of the most vulnerable of our world.

I grieve for a young tree, but my deeper grief is for what we are doing to our precious Earth and the suffering caused to all living beings. As Christopher Fry's poem says

> ... It takes
> So many thousand years to wake,
> But will you wake for pity's sake![46]

---

[45] Rabindranath Tagore, *Gitanjali XX*, The Lotus, on https://www.poetryverse.com/rabindranath-tagore-poems/the-lotus. The poem has a very encouraging ending: all is not lost in our absent mindedness.

[46] *A Sleep of Prisoners*, op. cit.

Cosmic Eucharist

I

This –
My Body –
a story
within a story
within a story
within a story
from the
Heart of the Fire
through the
Heart of the Fire
to the
Unknown
Unknowable
birthing
flaring forth
the Heart of the Fire
into an
explosion of
creative energy
a dance
a song of
galaxies
stars
black holes
super nova –
My Body –
the story of
beginnings
without endings
ever new strands
emerging within
the ancient new
tale
from the
Heart of the Fire

II

This –
My Body –
conceived
birthed from
dancing stars
in the
Heart of the Fire
fierce hot
molten mass
set spinning
in orbit
forming
solid crust
heaving up
mountains
carving out valleys
gathering
waters in
rivers and
oceans.
A single cell
births life
algae fungi
mosses grasses
herbs trees
fish reptiles
birds mammals
each depending
on all
one living
organism –
My Body –
from the
Heart of the Fire.

III

This –
My Body –
promethean
ancestors
taming
primordial fear
tamed
primordial
fire
into tribal
gathering
hearth-circles
birthing
Words
vehicle for
story telling
wisdom sharing
harnessing
purifying
transforming
power
to
fire and
melt and
mould a
new world –
My Body –
from the
Heart of the Fire

Dying to Live

IV

This –
My Body –
warmed by
heat from the
Heart of the Fire
two-edged sword
the heat
the fire
the power
unleashing
insatiably hungry
creative
destructive
Passion
breeding
weapons of war
wielded by
brother and
sister
destroying
brother and
sister
human and
other than human.
Yet
in the midst of
the heat of
the fire of
battle
the passion of
compassion
justice-making
reaches out
to heal
this –
My Body –
in the Heart of the Fire.

V

This –
My Body –
longing
yearning
seeking
I know not what
in the
Heart of the
Fire
that burns in
my heart
my gut
my thirst
locked in
combat with
fear
lust
power
control
for
independence
protecting
my separate self
separately.
Yet always
the lure
of the Song
of the
Heart of the
Fire:
Come
take my yoke
be consumed
in the
Heart of the Fire –
My Body.

VI

This Bread –
My Body –
in a time
before a time
a woman
took
sun-ripened
grain
ground it
on rock
mixed it
with water
kneading
a dough
consigned
it to the
Heart of the Fire
holding
all the ancient
stories
the joys
the griefs
the hopes
the anxieties
back to the
Unknown
Unknowable.
The dough
absorbing
absorbed by
the Heart of
the Fire,
born Bread –
this Bread –
My Body
broken for
You.
Take and eat.

VII

This –
My Blood –
warm with
heat from the
Heart of the Fire
lunar tides
ebb and flow
in ocean
in woman
in torrential
rains drained
in drought
spilt on
battlefield
in death
birthing life
in the
Heart of the Fire
coursing
through veins
and vines
made fertile
by decay
by pollens
borne by breeze
and bees
gathered
and crushed
in agony
turned ecstasy
in the Heart of the
Fire
This –
My Blood.

VIII

This –
My Blood –
passion
ignited from
the Heart of the
Fire
flaring forth
in desire that
turned inward
or outward
devours
or saves
unites
or divides
violates
or cares
two-edged sword
that attacks
or defends
spells life
in death
lights billions
of stars
and rocks
a new-born
in gentle arms.
Passions' harvests
tipped into vats
crushed
three days
left for dead
in the Heart of
the Fire.

◇◇◇

Wisdom
sets her table
and from
the Heart of
the Fire brings
forth
fine strained
wine –
this Cup –
My Blood
poured out for
you
Take and
drink...
if you dare.

2
Drawn toward the future

As our 2015 chapter approached, I knew the time was coming to retire from involvement in our congregational governance. The previous decade had been an exciting and challenging journey. Aware that we were an aging group, we set up a mission entity, Highways and Byways, so that our mission could continue beyond the life of the Missionary Sisters of Service. We also worked towards handing over our governance and administration to lay people.

A couple of months before the end of our term of office, our leadership team – Stancea, Bernadette and I – took a day to discern where each of us was, regarding a future role in MSS governance as this term came to an end. We invited Jill McCorquodale to facilitate the process:

> *Jill started us with the labyrinth this morning, following its intricate path to the centre, the God-space within, the ear of the heart, the place of inner listening. There I find an emptiness, a place of not-knowing. I also find a yearning without knowing for what. Only the Infinite can satisfy infinite emptiness.*
>
> *Paradoxically, at the same time I am conscious of fulness – of life, of grace, of giftedness, of gratitude, a fulness that comes from, and evokes, the YES spoken in my deepest self: a yes to life! a yes to mission! and not necessarily to any particular expression of these.*

Next, Jill invited us to pick three cards blindly, turn them over and take the one that drew our attention:

> *The card that drew me was of a chaotic vortex that suggested birthing, agony screaming in a powerful spiral energy that could also be the birth of the Cosmos. The words that came as I sat with the image were:*

> *Sent forth*
> *forming the far reaches of the Universe*
> *to be what is not yet.* 4.11.2015

While I could draw no clear direction from this, a few weeks earlier I had written:

> *I sense a shift in myself, a readiness to let go the many involvements of MSS governance and the board of Highways and Byways.[47] It isn't that I have lost interest or the passion, but I am not as attached, or perhaps as identified with them.* 27.10.2015

The French have a saying, 'Partir – c'est mourir un peu' - 'To leave is to die a little'. Leaving my involvements on the leadership team felt a bit like that. One of our sisters asked me if I was disappointed about not being elected to the incoming governing body:

> *I said 'No', but as I sit with that reality now, I feel a sense of loss in letting go that level of involvement – not so much letting go of the role, but the experience of being part of a small, dynamic team in which we could dream and explore together, re-imagining our future. I personally grow and my creativity is drawn forth in the process. That has been the extraordinary gift of our working together.* 28.11.2015

Retirement from office is not retirement from life. I looked forward to a more contemplative pace of life. Yet, as I reflect on that desire, I see that, even in my years of full engagement in various works, I experienced so much growth and contemplative insight. Perhaps contemplation is not so much about spending hours in prayer and meditation as it is about living our moment-to-moment experiences contemplatively. Of course, in order to live contemplatively, I do

---

47 *Highways and Byways: Healing the Land – Healing Ourselves – Together* is the mission entity established by the Missionary Sisters of Service to continue and extend their mission.

need to spend time in contemplative prayer each day. But growth in communion and wisdom do not depend on that alone.

Retirement also freed me for other involvements. For a number of years, I had been leading reflective reading groups on the Qur'an and the Bhagavad Gita at the Janssen Spirituality Centre.[48] While no scholar of Islam or Hinduism, I found that the experiece of our shared contemplative reading of their Scriptures opened in us an appreciation of those traditions, their people and cultures. The wisdom of those sacred texts often shone new light on our understanding of our own Scriptures and traditions.

I also came to appreciate more deeply that the Spirit of Wisdom is present in all faith traditions, drawing all into the same reality, the Divine, and the communion of all beings in One Sacred Mystery. This was way beyond the confines of what I was taught in my youth, that the Catholic Church is the only true church, the custodian of Divine revelation. No. All religious and indigenous traditions are custodians of Divine revelation, each according to its culture and history. We need the wisdom of all to come to the fulness of Divine revelation.

In February 2016, I participated in an interfaith pilgrimage in India. Its purpose, as articulated by its leader, Fr John Dupuche, was:

> To visit religious sites that are sacred to Islam, Hinduism, Buddhism and Christianity, to study texts from sacred writings, to discuss points of agreement and disagreement and so sense the religious experience that is proper to these faiths. In this way, members of the group will truly meet each other in spirit.

In the two weeks we were away, we visited the cities of Delhi, Varanasi, Bod Gaya and Kolkata. Our time was packed with experiences from early morning until the evening. I had no time to write my journal. All I managed to do before going to bed was to write a few brief notes on where we had been and what we done. Later on, when I had time to reflect, I wrote the story of the pilgrimage, using my

---

[48] The Janssen Spirituality Centre is dedicated to interfaith and intercultural relationship and runs a variety of programs and events to this purpose. Its website: https://www.janssencentre.org/.

sketchy notes. When I had completed it, I realised the value of having done so. The writing enabled me to absorb the pilgrimage experience at a deeper level. Had I not written it while the memories were fresh, I suspect much of the experience would have been lost to me.

Among my many memorable experiences, one that affected me most was our visit to Nirma Hriday, the home for the dying homeless, established by Mother Teresa of Kolkata and run by her sisters with the help of volunteers. Earlier in our pilgrimage in Varanashi, we attended the Agni Puja, a fire and light ceremony performed at sunset on the banks of the Ganges. Afterwards, walking back to the hotel where we were staying, the street was crowded with stalls, with people wanting to sell us things, and many people begging. I found it overwhelming. Not knowing how to be in that situation, I avoided looking at them. At the same time, I felt I was betraying some deeply held truth within myself. Perhaps it was something like Peter felt after his denial of knowing Jesus. Yet I didn't know what else I could do.

Then, at Nirma Hriday, we visited people who had been picked up off the streets. The Sister who welcomed us said to us: 'What these people need most is to know they are loved'. The women's ward, where I went, was spotless and very sparse: bare concrete walls and floor, a chair between each bed, all the beds made up with identical blue sheets, the women dressed alike in simple blue gowns. A serene peace pervaded the atmosphere. I spent some time with each woman I came to. I could not speak her language. I could only communicate by gesture. I simply held her hand and gave her my full attention.

Mid-afternoon, John celebrated Eucharist for the community and for us pilgrims. The others of our group did not want to go back to the ward after that, but I felt there was something more that this experience was meant to bring me.

When I re-entered the ward, some of the women were lying down, resting. I sat down on the edge of one woman's bed and gently stroked her arm from her shoulder down. With that, she rolled herself onto my lap and into my arms. I held her like a baby, her heart against my heart. I felt an amazing depth of love between us. I realised she was the same as the begging people I couldn't look at in Varanasi. And now, this gift of love: pure grace.

Seven years have elapsed since that experience and today I still feel moved by the gift of that encounter. I don't know the woman's name or whether she is still alive, but some part of her will always remain embedded in me.

◇◇◇

At our 2018 Chapter–Assembly, we celebrated a simple, yet powerful, ritual signifying our handing over responsibilities for mission to our lay partners in their various roles: Board members and Executive Officer, Stewardship Council members, and a number of other people involved in various ways with our community and its mission.

> *Many beautiful moments marked our days. The most powerfully poignant was the anointing ritual, anointing the non-professed of the community for mission and, while they anointed us, preparing beforehand the MSS body for burial (cf. Mark 14:8) While we Missionary Sisters of Service anointed each of them, the following passage from the Gospel was read*:
>
>> Jesus, with the power of the Spirit in him, returned to Galilee. He came to Nazara and went into the synagogue on the Sabbath day as he usually did. He stood up to read. Unrolling the scroll, he found the place where it is written:
>>
>>> The spirit of the Lord is on me, for he has anointed me
>>> to bring the good news to the afflicted.
>>> He has sent me to proclaim liberty to captives,
>>> sight to the blind, to let the oppressed go free,
>>> to proclaim a year of favour from the Lord.
>>
>> He then rolled up the scroll, gave it back to the assistant and sat down. Then he began to speak to them, 'This text is being fulfilled today even while you are listening' (Luke 4:14-21).

The ritual encapsulated the heart of the present phase of MSS: 'It is for your good that I go...' (John 16:7). It made real the urgency of self-surrender, emptying ourselves of all vestiges of clinging to the charism[49] that has formed us and our mission, trusting the Holy Spirit to do in those so called what the Spirit has been doing in us over the seventy-five plus years of our history.   28.10.2019

Although I had prepared this ritual, I was surprised at how deeply it moved me. As I anointed each person, I experienced conferring on him or her the MSS charism for mission. All of them had journeyed with us for several years or longer. They had been captured by our spirit of mission and had the commitment and competence to guide that mission now and into the future. The anointing signified our confidence in them and in the Spirit's promise to guide them in their mission.

After this anointing, our newly anointed lay partners anointed us Missionary Sisters of Service. Again I felt the power of this anointing, sealing the direction we were taking, of stepping back from holding the full responsibility of our charism and mission, gracing me personally, and us as a congregation, to let go graciously. With it, I knew my work as a member of the Highways and Byways board was completed. It was time to resign. I wrote my letter of resignation, conscious of Jesus saying to his disciples: 'It is for your own good that I go' (John 16:7). It was for the good of the Board and the future of Highways and Byways that we MSS withdraw so that they could take up our *charism* as truly their own.

A few days after this Assembly I received a letter that warmed my heart. Gabrielle McMullen, writing on behalf of the Stewardship Council, thanked me for the anointing ritual. She confirmed what I had experienced so powerfully, describing it as 'a defining and hope-filled moment... taking the MSS mission purposely into the future'.

I reflected again on the conception of the ritual. I had agreed to prepare a ritual on baptism as the call to mission, but I was at a

---

49 The *charism* is the gift of the Holy Spirit that characterises the particular spirit and vision for mission of a person or a community.

loss about just how to celebrate this in a meaningful ritual. Then, in the hours of the night, in that zone between sleeping and waking, a direction came to me. Working on it the next day, I had a strong sense of being guided as I shaped this ritual. Surely, the Spirit of God was and is at work among us!

3
Love does such things

When you remain silent from the thinking and willing of self, the eternal hearing, seeing and speaking will be revealed to you.[50]

The experiences and reflections that fill my journals of the decade from 2010 on, show a growing awareness of the astonishing and unconditional Love of God at the heart of all being and becoming. In Love, God pours out God*self* in the creation of the Universe. Richard Rohr calls this the first incarnation. Divine Love poured itself out anew, emptying itself to become part of Love's own creation, in the person of Jesus. And as if that is not enough, we see the extent to which Love is prepared to go as Jesus pours out his life on the cross. 'Greater love than this no one has...' (John 15:13). Love outpoured, emptied in self-giving, and poured out anew in the Holy Spirit who has been given to us (Romans 5:5): this the pattern that creates and sustains the Universe. This is also its salvation – and it is our mission.

While it is personal and immediate, the Spirit's love is cosmic, as Ilia Delio writes:

> Love is what makes the world go 'round. It is fundamental to the forward movement of evolution... By the sheer power of its energy, love draws everything into an endless depth of greater wholeness. On the level of human consciousness, the core energy of personal/sexual love must reach out to the wider realm of humanity that includes love of neighbour, friendship and love of stranger. Love, sex and cosmic evolution are intertwined in a field of integral wholeness; to deny, avoid or negate any of them is to thwart the process of deepening life.[51]

---

50 Jacob Boehme, *Way to Christ*, p.171, quoted by Cynthia Bourgeault in *The Holy Trinity and the Law of Three*, op. cit.
51 Ilia Delio, *The Unbearable Wholeness of Being*, Orbis Books, Maryknoll NY. P. 51

This cosmic dimension of human-Divine love is beautifully imaged by Cynthia Bourgeault in a passage in *The Holy Trinity and the Law of Three*:

> In that garden on Easter morning, as she (Mary Magdalen) receives Jesus' request, 'Do not cling to me for I have not yet ascended to the Father', (he) gently widens the space... Without losing any of its human particularity, their love becomes vast and luminous throughout the Cosmos, drawing together all of those realms visible and invisible in a single sacred embrace that indeed bears within it the fullness of the Mercy of God.[52]

Cynthia names this love 'the immortal diamond[53] fused at the very heart of the density of this world.' This immortal diamond is within me, within all of us. Its transforming power can only be realised when we empty ourselves in self-giving, as Jesus emptied himself on the cross and as Mary Magdalen was emptied as she stood by his cross and wept by his grave. Cynthia claims that this transformation is the purpose for which we are created, and that we 'are required to offer (it) back to the cosmos on the altar of our own transfigured hearts'.[54]

It is almost ten years since I first read Cynthia's description of this Easter morning encounter between Jesus and Mary Magdalen. I have gone back to it many times since. It sets my heart burning. Yet, for this spaciousness to happen in my relationship with Christ, I must *walk out the gate naked*, as I heard years earlier. Many layers need to be stripped off (ouch!) before I can truly walk naked, as the immortal diamond of love which is my true Self, open to the world, to the Cosmos. And it cannot happen without suffering:

> *I listened to a conversation on The Cost of True Love between Cynthia Bourgeault and Ilia Delio. It spoke to*

---

52 Cynthia Bourgeault, *The Holy Trinity* op. cit. p. 168.
53 Richar Rohr often likens True Self to a diamond buried deep within us, formed under the intense pressure of our lives, that must be searched for, uncovered, and separated from all the debris of ego that surrounds it. See his book, *Immortal Diamond*, Jossey-Bass, 2012.
54 Bourgeault, op. cit.

what I found when working on my early journals and the pain and suffering expressed there. As I keep pondering those experiences, I sense there is something profoundly sacred happening in these pages, though I didn't know it at the time. In my prayer this morning I experienced that suffering is the hidden face of love. It is Love stripping away all that mars love's full expression. It is the dying to the egoic self that Love may be living fully in and through me, reaching out through me to the world around me.
23.2.2020

Is it because we human beings try to avoid suffering, that *hidden face of love*, that violence is sweeping the world with seeming new intensity? Daily the media headlines news of wars and of groups or individuals lighting spot fires of terror anywhere in the world:

The response of governments seems, on the whole, to fight fire with fire, terror with terror, violence with violence, death and destruction with death and destruction. This is about as effective as fighting a bushfire with petrol! In the midst of this world's reality, Pope Francis has called for a Holy Year of Mercy: 'to rediscover and make fruitful the mercy of God with which all of us are called to give consolation to every man and woman (and child) of our time'.
21.11.2015

I like the Dutch word for mercy, *barmhartigheid*. *Barm* is yeast; *hartigheid* means heartedness or heartiness. Yeast needs warmth to leaven the dough. The yeast of Divine Mercy needs the warmth of our human hearts to do its work in the world. My reflection takes me back to Cynthia Bourgeault's, *The Holy Trinity and the Law of Three*:

Cynthia identifies the fruit of Oneness, Love and Word (of the Blessed Trinity) as Mercy, Barmhartigheid. She sees Mercy as 'the most primary element of all that is beyond the inner life of the Divine Mystery... It is at the core of all things, the wellspring of being, and is what Merton is describing when he writes, 'The core of life that exists in all

> *things is tenderness, mercy, virginity, the light'.*[55] *If this is so, the more we come back to our deepest truth, back to who and what we essentially are, the more fully we will **be** that tender mercy and compassion.*   3.12.2015

Divine Mercy, that most foundational element of all that is, is what unites and enlivens all creation as one, with the same oneness as that of the Blessed Trinity. I like to think of Divine Mercy as the DNA of the Cosmos, the DNA of our DNA. The Divine Heart of Mercy and Compassion for the whole of creation and every individual being within it beats in our human hearts. If only we could realise that!

My journals show a growing consciousness of the Cosmos as a community of beings. I am not just an individual. I am part of a family and community, the community of all beings, not only biologically, but essentially. It is who and what I am, who and what we are:

> *The Mystery that births the Universe is so vast, so utterly beyond us, yet so personally intimate, the Being of all Being and beings. It is our oneness with each other – the Unbearable Wholeness that bears me as immediately as it bears the Whole – the energy of Love. It is the fire Jesus came to cast upon the Earth, and, with him, I long for it to be enkindled! But that requires me also to go through his baptism.*   26.8.2017

That Love is the mission Jesus entrusted to the disciples, a love that is always ready to reach out to others, a love that is not afraid to be vulnerable with the vulnerable. Reflecting on Jesus washing the feet of his disciples:

> *'He removed his outer garments...' (John 13: 4). There is a profound intimacy in washing someone's feet. A condition for that intimacy is to be naked in meeting the other, laying down one's outer garment of role or status, simply being oneself without pretence or pretentiousness. It means being vulnerable to the other, no defences, simply being*

---
55 Cynthia Bourgeault, *The Holy Trinity*, op.cit. p. 150.

with the other as I am. It is so simple. Why is it so difficult? As John Powell's friend said, 'You may not like who I truly am, and it's all I've got'. But that's the risk of loving.
11.5.2017

I grew up with the understanding that the Church's mission was to convert people 'to the Faith'. This was understood as bringing them into the Catholic fold. Over the years I have come to a broader understanding of our mission. It is a mission to so live in love that people will be drawn to the One from whom all love comes. It makes me wonder:

> *What if we, the Church, got it all wrong? We have come to assume that the Gospel mission is to 'compel them to come in that my house may be full' (Luke 14:23). What if that 'house' was never meant to be the Church as we know it? What if, rather, our mission of love is to be leaven in the world (cf. Matthew 13:33), of forgiving, compassionate love for every creature? A love that seeks justice, to do justice; a love that seeks to understand the human heart of friend and 'enemy'; a love that reaches beyond fear, rage and violence; a love that is the oil of healing and empowering in a new birth; the Love that 'renews the face of the Earth', the face of religion – Christian, Muslim, Hindu, Buddhist, Jew, etc. – of all people formed by and in other religions and spiritual traditions, atheists, and adherents of the multitudes of 'isms'...*   18.6.2014

The reflection continues a few days later:

> *I keep thinking about the Gospel imperative of love that is all inclusive, with no strings attached; to be that love in the world like leaven in dough, working in a hidden way until it permeates the whole mass, making it light and flexible, generating trust and hope robust enough to deal with pain, dysfunction, failure, betrayal, violence, wars, etc. and not to be destroyed by those evils...*   23.6.2014

And not be destroyed by those evils?

> *This morning, looking at the crucifix, I 'heard': No matter what you do to me, or to my Body, my love is unconditional. Can I love so unconditionally no matter who this brother or sister and what they may or may not do? This is enormously challenging. But God's grace and mercy has been, and continues to be, poured into our hearts by the Holy Spirit given to us. I have experienced that unconditional love expressed in myself. I don't know it is in me, but it comes alive when I am with others or when I hear of troubles and tragedies that wound people or cause them to wound others. I long to pour that love on their wounds, to make my heart a refuge for them, where they can be embraced by love, just as they are.* 29.12.2020

I notice how, over the years, that mission has also become my prayer. Often, as I begin my prayer, I cast my mind over the world and hold its suffering peoples in my heart, in the tenderness of Divine Mercy. I have no words in such prayer. I am simply there, present to the Mystery that holds us all, and the whole of creation, in one embrace of Love, Mercy, Barmhartigheid.

Before I began to glimpse these things, it never occurred to me that there is a *cosmic* dimension to our lives and relationships. But whenever we encounter another in self-giving love, its ripples go out to the ends of the world. This is the work of the Spirit in and through us. It is the mission I was born for, long before I embraced the *mission of love and service on the highways and byways* of life as a Missionary Sister of Service. It is the mission of every person and community on this Earth, if only we recognised this.

Mid-2016, I made a month-long retreat, in Rhyll on Phillip Island, in the home of Gabrielle and John Mahony who were away for a month. The serenity of their home and its surroundings made for a beautiful retreat venue. Yet I found this retreat very challenging. Times of sitting still to pray or meditate seemed to drag endlessly. One day, it dawned on me afresh:

> *Reflecting on my dryness in prayer and my lack of any sense of God or faith, it struck me: Of course! If God is Unfathomable, Unknowable Mystery, Emptiness that is*

> *Fecund Fulness, how can we expect to encounter I AM in our limited sensory way? So, darkness and dryness in prayer, the sense of the absence of God, is not just about purification so we can once again experience God as light. It is the very nature of encounter with the One who is beyond all knowing.* 25.5.2016

I have had to learn this truth over and over again. The Divine invitation is simply to rest in the Silence and the absent Presence of the Silent One. In that resting I discover anew that:

> *Emptiness is the womb of fullness; darkness is the womb of light; silence is the womb of sound...*

The positive cannot exist except for the negative that holds it. I saw it so clearly in that moment. Yet still, to remain in the darkness, the emptiness, the eternal silence is so... well... empty!

Day after day of that retreat, I sat before the crucifix, conscious of the intense suffering of Jesus, abandoned, so it seemed, even by his Father. He too experienced that emptiness:

> Who, though he was divine,
> did not cling to his equality with God
> but emptied himself, taking the form of a slave,
> born in human likeness, like us in all things...
> He humbled himself still more,
> becoming obedient unto death,
> even death on a cross. (cf. Philippians 2:5-8)

How well I knew this hymn from Philippians! I had been drawn back to it again and again over the years. And still – how difficult I found it to sit in my own emptiness before the crucifix. Then, one day I was shown something so profound, its impact shaped my inner life from that day on:

> *My prayer today has been focused on the crucifix. I read somewhere of a Rabbi who visited a Catholic Church. After looking at the crucifix for a few minutes, he said something like, 'I could never be part of a religion that*

> *has such a violent image as its focus?. I asked myself, what do I see as I look at the crucifix? 'He emptied himself...' I see Love pouring out himself to the last drop of his blood. Love is only possible when we empty ourselves. Meister Eckhart says, when we empty ourselves, God can't not come in.*   31.5.2016

Of course, this insight wasn't new to me. But this time it hit me with an immediacy that changed my life: It was – and is – the outpouring of Divine Love to the last drop of Jesus' blood, for the life of the world. It was thus from the very beginning. Creation itself is God's Love and Mercy outpouring itself in the ever-increasing diversity of the self-creating Universe. In the Christ on the Cross, I saw the entire Divine Mystery, from the Trinity to incarnation as creation, to the Christ incarnate in Jesus, to us and on to 'the fullness of God' to which we are constantly being drawn. Divine Mercy is like a great river, forever flowing, creating and drawing all into its life-giving waters. Words can't do justice to the Mystery. It is full of paradox.

> *Sitting before the crucifix, I am confronted by paradox: the Infinite manifesting in a limited human body; the One who is Life subjected to death; the creator murdered by his creatures: 'He emptied himself'. . . The Crucified One tells me that to become fully human I need to empty myself to make space for others and THE Other. I can only do that by the grace of the Spirit in me. Its fruits are love, peace, and joy in abundance – sheer grace!*   1.6.2016

It is not enough that I contemplate this Mystery in Christ. I am called to live it; to live with my arms outstretched wide, as Christ stretched out his arms on the Cross, totally empty of anything and everything I might cling to, so that the same fullness of Divine Love and Mercy can flow as freely through me as it flows through the Crucified One – for the Life of the world, of the Cosmos and every being in it. It calls me to embrace every being as Christ embraces them, to heal, to restore, to bring them to fullness of life. It can only be so at the cost of my life. It is *walking out of the gate naked*, that invitation that continually calls me into new depths.

These insights had been building up in me over many years, back to that retreat in Hobart many decades earlier, when I 'heard': *and the Word was made flesh and her name was Corrie*. I realised back then that we had not even begun to explore the depth of the mystery of the incarnation. As I look back, it seems that my life since has been shaped by that exploration. Whenever I received a further glimpse into the mystery, it usually came with new immediacy in my experience of the Crucified One. Looking back, I can see its slow transforming grace at work in me, not by my doing, but by the Spirit of the One who pours himself out in tender Love and Mercy, for the life of the world. Stupendous Mystery of Love! And it is all there, in the Crucified One.

4
Unfinished symphony

The time will come
When, with elation,
you will greet yourself arriving
at your own door, in your own mirror,
and each will smile at the other's welcome

and say, sit here. Eat.
You will love again the stranger who was your self.
Give wine. Give bread. Give back your heart
to itself, to the stranger who has loved you

all your life, whom you ignored
for another, who knows you by heart.
Take down the love letters from the bookshelf,

the photographs, the desperate notes,
peel your image from the mirror.
Sit. Feast on your life.

— Derek Walcott[56]

It is time to bring to a close this unfinished tale. Four years ago, when I embarked on the venture of writing my story, I had no idea of the journey it would take me on. My plan was to read my journals, identify significant experiences and weave my story from these. It didn't take long before I realised it wasn't going to work like that.

Reading and reflecting on my journals has been something of a pilgrimage for me, an amazing journey. Meeting myself at less than half my current age brought many surprises. One of these was discovering that, in all my dark, confusing times, Wisdom was secretly at work, creating a work of art out of the messiness of my life. It seems that it is precisely in the experience of brokenness, weakness and vulnerability, that God enters without our knowing it. As Leonard

---

56 Derek Walcott, *Love After Love*, https://allpoetry.com/love-after-love.

Cohan's song expresses so powerfully: *There is a crack in everything: that's how the light gets in*. With St Paul, I can rejoice in my weaknesses and failures, knowing that Grace finds its full strength in weakness (cf. 2 Corinthians 12:9).

I have sometimes been asked for whom I am writing this book. When I began it, the question had not occurred to me. But the further I got into the journey, the more I realised that I needed to write it for myself. Those journals hold a wisdom that I had not recognised when I wrote them. It needed the perspective of years to enable me to discover it. Two or three years into the project, on one of my early morning walks, I 'heard': 'It takes a lifetime to grow up'. As I registered what I heard, I laughed: 'I hope I live long enough!' My journals record that process of growing up.

I mentioned earlier that an Aboriginal Elder once said to me: 'You'll never know who you are until you go back to your own country'. In my reading of my journals, pondering what I read, then writing the story of my life, I have been on my own country and lived intimately with it. In the process, my identity, which was such a big issue in earlier years, has melted into a much larger identity: it is no longer about me as this individual called Corrie. It is about me as an infinitesimal, yet precious part of the Divine Mystery, incarnate in Christ, incarnate in all creation on its evolutionary journey to ever greater fullness of being. That's where I belong, where I am at home, where my mission is.

I turn again to the poet Tagore:

> On the day when the lotus bloomed, alas,
> my mind was straying, and I knew it not.
> My basket was empty and the flower remained unheeded.
>
> Only now and again a sadness fell upon me,
> and I started up from my dream
> and felt a sweet trace of a strange fragrance in the south wind.
>
> That vague sweetness made my heart ache with longing
> and it seemed to me that it was
> the eager breath of the summer seeking for its completion.

I knew not then that it was so near,
that it was mine,
and that this perfect sweetness had blossomed
in the depth of my own heart.[57]

That was my life journey. While I was going about my ordinary daily life, unbeknown to me, the One who is mighty was doing great things in me. I needed to write this story. I needed to read and ponder my journals to discover that, what I had longed for all my life was, all the time, growing within me.

Happy the day I first picked up a pen to write a journal! It was the key to my secret inner world. Writing became a way of listening to my heart and my feelings. It gave me a language in which I could express what I heard and felt. Even today, I am astounded by what I find in those journals. This isn't my story. It is the story of God's working in my life. Amazing grace!

While I bring this story to a close, I am aware, as the writer of John's Gospel says, there are many other things that happened that are not written in this book. But, as the song says, 'this much is ready now'.[58] It is my hope and prayer that my journal journey may serve as something of a mirror in which readers may recognise more deeply the Spirit's working in their own lives.

---

57 Tagore, *Gitanjali, The Lotus*, op cit.
58 Joe Wise, *Here is my Life*, https://www.youtube.com/watch?v=Ao5VnopCP-Y

Postscript
Gratitude, gratitude, ever more gratitude

How do I begin to express the enormous debt I owe for my life? My primary gratitude, of course, goes to the One who wrote this story in my life. This book is first of all the story of grace, of God's gracious working in my life and in all that has supported and sustained me since before the world was made. Only secondarily is it *my* story.

Next, my gratitude goes to my parents, Nic and Corrie van den Bosch, through whom I came into this world and who, in the family they lovingly raised, laid the foundations for what my life has become. I am also deeply grateful to my community of Missionary Sisters of Service and its founder, Father John C. Wallis. Participating in the life and mission of the congregation, and with the support I received from our shared journey, the raw material I was when I joined has become finely honed. John often encouraged us to look at big maps. When I came to the congregation in 1959, the map of my inner and outer worlds was very small indeed. Exposure to people, places, ideas and mentors have continually stretched those maps and helped me situate myself in them. Thank you, Sisters. Thank you also to John and those of our sisters who have completed the earthly phase of their journey and who continue to be a source of inspiration for me.

To the people I have lived and worked among on the highways and byways of life and mission, all of whom, in one way or another, have left their mark on my life: Thank you.

I have had many gurus along the way, mostly as writers in theology and spirituality, literature, cosmology, and so on, whose works came along just when I was ready for them. Many of my journal entries are reflections on what I was reading, particularly when these throw a light on what I was experiencing or questioning. They have contributed greatly to stretching my maps. I notice that in earlier years, they were predominantly male authors. But over the past thirty years or so, it was more often the writings of women theologians and spiritual journeyers that lit the way for me.

Then there are the other kind of wisdom writers, the poets. Their poems often express profound insights I struggle to find words for. My gratitude goes to them all. They have become part of my story, and without them, I could not have come to the understanding of my life that I now have.

At about the halfway point of writing this book, I was wondering whether this was going to be of any interest to anyone besides myself. About that time, I watched a conversation on mysticism between Robert Ellsberg, editor in chief of Orbis Books, and Mirabai Starr, whose writings I love. I wondered, would Robert be someone who could give me some objective feedback? Feeling rather audacious, I wrote and asked him. To my delight, he graciously agreed to do so. I sent him what I had written up to that point, suggesting he might just like to read a few pages here and there to get a sense of the work. Two weeks later I received his response. It was evident that he had read the whole document. He thanked me for sharing it with him, calling it 'a remarkable document—beautifully written, deeply honest and revealing. I agree with you that it is not just a personal story, but a story of Grace. I am glad you have done this.' I was blown away by those generous and encouraging comments. I returned to my writing with renewed energy. Thank you, Robert.

To those who have read drafts along the way: my sister Jose Kristensen, my dear friends, Fran Spora, Liz McAloon, and proof-readers Joan Kenny and Fiona Basile: your feedback and encouragement meant a lot. A very special thanks to Madeline Duckett rsm and Brian Gallagher msc, who read the work with loving and receptive hearts and generous comments. All their contributions have helped the final editing of the book.

Lastly, my gratitude to the publishers. When I first contacted Hugh McGinlay at Coventry Press, he looked at a sample chapter and the number of words in the manuscript and commented on the length of the book. In print, it would amount to about 400 pages. Such a volume, and by an unknown writer, would make it a hard book to sell. Could I make it shorter? It seemed like a big ask, but as I reworked the draft, I was able to sharpen its focus. I think the book is the better for it. Thank you, Hugh.

And so, I come back to the One without whom there would be no book, no story, no Corrie, and I sing with Mary:

My soul rings out the glory of the Lord
And my spirit rejoices in God my saviour!
For the One who is mighty has done great things in me:
Holy is God's name!

Appendix
The Missionary Sisters of Service story

The story begins in 1933 on Bruny Island, Tasmania. Father John Wallis, 23 years old and newly ordained, was on a mission to people on Bruny Island, travelling by bicycle, horseback and on foot, visiting isolated families. The island was rarely visited by a priest, and young John was determined to seek out as many people as he could during his short time there. In the course of his visits, he met a mother, Mrs Kit Hawkins, who said to him, 'Father, what about us? Why can't we have Sisters to teach our children? Doesn't anyone care about us in the bush?' John listened compassionately, but had no answer for her.

Kit's question was a challenge that John could not let go. Over the next ten years he pondered, prayed, talked and wrote about the needs of people 'out beyond'. Gradually an idea formed in his mind: a community of women whose mission would be to go into the highways and byways of rural and outback Australia, seeking out people 'beyond'.

In 1943, at a meeting of the Legion of Mary in Burnie, John spoke about the needs of people of the bush and his 'dream' for a community of women to meet that need. Among those present, one woman, Gwen Morse, was touched by John's words. Her heart responded: she felt a call. She contacted him a day or two later, and offered herself for his vision. In Hobart, several more women heard that call and offered themselves.

In July 1944, four women came together in Launceston, Tasmania: Gwen Morse (Sister Teresa), Kathleen Moore (Sister Vianney), Alice Carroll (Sister Monica), Joyce O'Brien (Sister Chanel), to be joined a few months later by two more: Valerie Casey (Sister Venard) and Agnes Ryan (Sister Magdalen). These were the founding community of the Home Missionary Sisters of Our Lady.

The community grew and developed its mission: its members were to be mobile, travelling to rural parishes, visiting families, instructing their children, preparing them for the sacraments and so on. They took with them books and reading material that could help people grow in their faith. They developed correspondence courses, so parents could instruct their own children. Over time, their mission grew and diversified in response to the needs of people they encountered.

Other areas of Australia called for their work. In 1957, the first group of Sisters moved beyond Tasmania, to the Wilcannia-Forbes Diocese, covering outback New South Wales, followed, in 1965, by a foundation in the Toowoomba Diocese, from where the sisters' work covered the vast south-west of Queensland. Then in 1971, the Diocese of Port Pirie, South Australia, welcomed its first Sisters. From their base in Whyalla, they travelled throughout the Eyre Peninsula and Inland as far as Central Australia.

As the community's sense of identity and the character of their mission developed, the congregation changed its title to better reflect their mission and vision. The new name, Missionary Sisters of Service, was adopted in 1971.

In response to the ever-growing geographical spread of the sisters and the needs of ongoing formation for their work, in 1983 the congregation moved its headquarters to Melbourne. Since then, their work and outreach has continued to grow, while no new women have come to join them.

Realising that the congregation is not going to live beyond the life of its current members, in 2010 the community set up a mission entity which enables the mission to grow and continue into the future. Initially named the John Wallis Foundation, it is now known as Highways and Byways – Healing the Land – Healing Ourselves – Together.